CLASSIC cafe

12 designs in **Cashsoft**
& **Cashcotton DK**
by Martin Storey

Welcome to Classic Cafe, the very first brochure in the RYC Classic Collection. We have designed this brand new collection of DK handknits with the mature but fashion-conscious knitter in mind. What we've devised is a look that has a delightful contemporary feel, yet will stand the test of time.

Shot on location in one of London's most fashionable high streets, Classic Cafe features a range of handknit designs that are a real pleasure to wear – whether for meeting friends for a relaxed coffee, for sunny-day picnics in the park, for walking the dog, or simply for a spot of leisurely window shopping.

Designs include: the witty Deli trellis trim cardigan coat, which takes its inspiration from couture classics; the must-have Manhattan fringe trim tailored jacket; the Broadway cable with its ageless versatility; and the Liberty stripe which is a tribute to the spirit of independence.

To accompany the Classic Cafe range, we bring you a duo of wonderfully luxurious yarns, especially developed by the Rowan design team.

As its name suggests, Cashsoft DK is a cosy cashmere/wool blend with a velvety feel, available in a palette of sumptuous summer colours including Bella Donna lilac, Sweet pink and Mirage blue.

In contrast, Cashcotton is a cashmere/cotton blend, available in a summer palette of cool shades such as Apple green, Magenta and Quartz.

Meticulously designed, the RYC Classic Collection of handknits is a joy to knit and a pleasure to wear. The versatility of these key handknit items means that each one will cleverly complement and enhance an existing wardrobe, adding a touch of creativity and freshness.

Classic Cafe features a range of handknit designs that are a real pleasure to wear – whether for meeting friends for a relaxed coffee, for sunny-day picnics in the park, for walking the dog, or simply for a spot of leisurely window shopping.

8 **Empire** in Cashsoft DK

10 **Plaza** in Cashcotton DK

22 **Broadway** in Cashsoft DK

24 **Tiffany** in Cashsoft DK

Empire – this Candelabra cable effect achieves a striking but feminine mood, enhanced by the silver bead "flame" detail. Fitted to the waist with a low crew neck, this sweater is a neat summer item.

Knitted in Cashsoft DK, shown here in Bella Donna 502 decorated with large clear beads J3001008. Pattern instructions page 56

Plaza – now for something quirky: this knitted jacket has crocheted corkscrew collar detailing. The elaborate detailing is set off by a neat fitted shape.

Knitted in Cashcotton DK, shown here in Apple 603. Pattern instructions page 50

Madison — this graphic stripe jacket, with its fold-down collar, looks great with a fashionably thin belt and a cheeky summer hat.

Knitted in Cashsoft DK,
shown here in Cream 500,
Ballad Blue 508 &
Black 519. Pattern
instructions page 46

Manhattan – here's the shapely jacket that we all need this summer. With its moss stitch, curvy outline and crochet fringing, it combines softness with a tailored look.

Knitted in Cashsoft DK, shown here in Bella Donna 502.
Pattern instructions page 48

Liberty – this colourful wrap-over cardigan has a smarter, café look with ties at the back and semi-fitted sleeves. It's knitted in a stripe and "pull-up" stitch that gives a subtle over-all texture.

Knitted in Cashsoft DK Mist 505 &Clemantine 510, Cashcotton DK Apple 603. Pattern instructions page 63

Deli – to make things go with a swing, wear this trellis trim-knit coat over a summer dress and stride out with confidence. The low neck is fastened with knitted cords.

Knitted in Cashcotton DK, shown here in Quartz 606. Pattern instructions page 40

Knitted in Cashsoft DK, shown here in Tape 515. Pattern instructions page 60

Broadway – highly versatile, this crop cabled jacket has a charming moss stitch collar. An item bound to become a favourite – and what could be better to wear for walking the dog!

Tiffany – wear this over-shirt, with its deep neckline, over a t-shirt or bikini top for a casual summer look. The crochet stitch creates a cool, crisp handle.

Knitted in Cashsoft DK, shown here in Mirage 503. Pattern instructions page 52

Hudson – no wardrobe is complete without a Hudson! For breezy spring days and summer evenings, this classic cable tunic works with everything – from a pair of jeans to a pretty print skirt.

Knitted in Cashsoft DK, shown here in Bella Donna 502. Pattern instructions page 42

Jersey (right)– a classic design updated, this design is inspired by the Breton sailor jumper. Wear it with a crisp white shirt and finish with a pretty knotted scarf.

Knitted in Cashsoft DK, shown here in Mirage 503 & Poppy 512. Pattern instructions page 44

Whitney – with its flattering Raglan sleeves and little rib pockets, this cardigan is the ultimate summer item.

Knitted in Cashsoft DK, shown here in Ballad Blue 508. Pattern instructions page 54

Hamilton – our subtly striped v-necked sweater is set off by a crochet trim to add a touch of femininity. You can add a corsage for effect.

Knitted in Cashsoft DK, shown here in Mist 505, Cream 500 &
Mirage 503. Pattern instructions page 58

Deli

Manhattan

Hudson

Jersey

Plaza

Tiffany

Liberty

Broadway

Madison

Hamilton

Whitney

Tension

Obtaining the correct tension is perhaps the single factor which can make the difference between a successful garment and a disastrous one. It controls both the shape and size of an article, so any variation, however slight, can distort the finished garment. Different designers feature in our books and it is **their** tension, given at the **start** of each pattern, which you must match. We recommend that you knit a square in pattern and/or stocking stitch (depending on the pattern instructions) of perhaps 5 - 10 more stitches and 5 - 10 more rows than those given in the tension note. Mark out the central 10cm square with pins. If you have too many stitches to 10cm try again using thicker needles, if you have too few stitches to 10cm try again using finer needles. Once you have achieved the correct tension your garment will be knitted to the measurements indicated in the size diagram shown at the end of the pattern.

Sizing and Size Diagram Note

The instructions are given for the smallest size. Where they vary, work the figures in brackets for the larger sizes. **One set of figures refers to all sizes.** Included with most patterns in this magazine is a '**size diagram**', or sketch of the finished garment and its dimensions. The size diagram shows the finished width of the garment at the under-arm point, and it is this measurement that the knitter should choose first; a useful tip is to measure one of your own garments which is a comfortable fit. Having chosen a size based on width, look at the corresponding length for that size; if you are not happy with the total length which we recommend, adjust your own garment before beginning your armhole shaping - any adjustment after this point will mean that your sleeve will not fit into your garment easily - don't forget to take your adjustment into account if there is any side seam shaping. Finally, look at the sleeve length; the size diagram shows the finished sleeve measurement, taking into account any top-arm insertion length. Measure your body between the centre of your neck and your wrist, this measurement should correspond to half the garment width plus the sleeve length. Again, your sleeve length may be adjusted, but remember to take into consideration your sleeve increases if you do adjust the length - you must increase more frequently than the pattern states to shorten your sleeve, less frequently to lengthen it.

Chart Note

Many of the patterns in the book are worked from charts. Each square on a chart represents a stitch and each line of squares a row of knitting. Each colour used is given a different letter and these are shown in the **materials** section, or in the **key** alongside the chart of each pattern. When working from the charts, read odd rows (K) from right to left and even rows (P) from left to right, unless otherwise stated.

Finishing Instructions

After working for hours knitting a garment, it seems a great pity that many garments are spoiled because such little care is taken in the pressing and finishing process. Follow the following tips for a truly professional-looking garment.

Pressing

Block out each piece of knitting and following the instructions on the ball band press the garment pieces, omitting the ribs. Tip: Take special care to press the edges, as this will make sewing up both easier and neater. If the ball band indicates that the fabric is not to be pressed, then covering the blocked out fabric with a damp white cotton cloth and leaving it to stand will have the desired effect. Darn in all ends neatly along the selvage edge or a colour join, as appropriate.

Stitching

When stitching the pieces together, remember to match areas of colour and texture very carefully where they meet. Use a seam stitch such as back stitch or mattress stitch for all main knitting seams and join all ribs and neckband with mattress stitch, unless otherwise stated.

Construction

Having completed the pattern instructions, join left shoulder and neckband seams as detailed above. Sew the top of the sleeve to the body of the garment using the method detailed in the pattern, referring to the appropriate guide:

Straight cast-off sleeves: Place centre of cast-off edge of sleeve to shoulder seam. Sew top of sleeve to body, using markers as guidelines where applicable.

Square set-in sleeves: Place centre of cast-off edge of sleeve to shoulder seam. Set sleeve head into armhole, the straight sides at top of sleeve to form a neat right-angle to cast-off sts at armhole on back and front.

Shallow set-in sleeves: Place centre of cast-off edge of sleeve to shoulder seam. Join cast-off sts at beg of armhole shaping to cast-off sts at start of sleeve-head shaping. Sew sleeve head into armhole, easing in shapings.

Set-in sleeves: Place centre of cast-off edge of sleeve to shoulder seam. Set in sleeve, easing sleeve head into armhole.

Join side and sleeve seams.
Slip stitch pocket edgings and linings into place. Sew on buttons to correspond with buttonholes. Ribbed welts and neckbands and any area of garter stitch should not be pressed.

Abbreviations

K	knit
P	purl
st(s)	stitch(es)
inc	increas(e)(ing)
dec	decreas(e)(ing)
st st	stocking stitch (1 row K, 1 row P)
g st	garter stitch (K every row)
beg	begin(ning)
foll	following
rem	remain(ing)
rev st st	reverse stocking stitch (1 row P, 1 row K)
rep	repeat
alt	alternate
cont	continue
patt	pattern
tog	together
mm	millimetres
cm	centimetres
in(s)	inch(es)
RS	right side
WS	wrong side
sl 1	slip one stitch
psso	pass slipped stitch over
tbl	through back of loop
M1	make one stitch by picking up horizontal loop before next stitch and working into back of it
moss st	row 1 (RS): K1, *P1, K1, rep from * to end. row 2: As row 1. these 2 rows form moss st.
yrn	yarn round needle
yfwd	yarn forward
yon	yarn over needle
meas	measures
o	no stitches, times or rows
-	no stitches, times or rows for that size

Crochet terms

UK crochet terms and abbreviation have been used throughout. The list below gives the US equivalent where they vary.

Abbrev.	UK	US
dc	double crochet	single crochet
htr	half treble	half double crochet
tr	treble	double crochet
dtr	double treble	treble

 = Easy, straight forward knitting

 = Suitable for the average knitter

Deli

YARN

	XS	S	M	L	XL	
To fit bust	81	86	91	97	102	cm
	32	34	36	38	40	in

RYC Cashcotton DK

| | 9 | 10 | 10 | 11 | 11 | x 50gm |

(photographed in Quartz 606)

NEEDLES

1 pair 4mm (no 8) (US 6) needles
Two double-pointed 3¼mm (no 10) (US 3) needles

TENSION

22 sts and 30 rows to 10 cm measured over stocking stitch using 4mm (US 6) needles.

BACK

Using 4mm (US 6) needles cast on 118 [124: 130: 136: 142] sts.
Beg with a K row, work in st st for 20 rows, ending with RS facing for next row.
Row 21 (dec) (RS): (K10, K2tog) twice, K to last 24 sts, (K2tog tbl, K10) twice.
Work 13 rows.
Rep last 14 rows 3 times more, then row 21 (the dec row) again. 98 [104: 110: 116: 122] sts.
Cont straight until back meas 42 [43: 43: 44: 44] cm, ending with RS facing for next row.
Shape armholes
Cast off 5 [6: 6: 7: 7] sts at beg of next 2 rows.
88 [92: 98: 102: 108] sts.
Dec 1 st at each end of next 5 [5: 7: 7: 9] rows, then on foll 1 [2: 2: 3: 3] alt rows, then on every foll 4th row until 72 [74: 76: 78: 80] sts rem.
Cont straight until armhole meas 20 [20: 21: 21: 22] cm, ending with RS facing for next row.
Shape shoulders and back neck
Cast off 7 sts at beg of next 2 rows.
58 [60: 62: 64: 66] sts.
Next row (RS): Cast off 7 sts, K until there are 10 [10: 11: 11: 12] sts on right needle and turn, leaving rem sts on a holder.
Work each side of neck separately.
Cast off 4 sts at beg of next row.
Cast off rem 6 [6: 7: 7: 8] sts.
With RS facing, rejoin yarn to rem sts, cast off centre 24 [26: 26: 28: 28] sts, K to end.
Complete to match first side, reversing shapings.

LEFT FRONT

Using 4mm (US 6) needles cast on 46 [49: 52: 55: 58] sts.
Beg with a K row, work in st st as folls:
Work 1 row, ending with **WS** facing for next row.
Inc 1 st at beg of next row and at same edge on foll 8 rows, then on foll 2 alt rows, then on foll 4th row. 58 [61: 64: 67: 70] sts.
Work 2 rows, ending with RS facing for next row.
Row 21 (dec) (RS): (K10, K2tog) twice, K to end.
Inc 1 st at front opening edge of next row.
57 [60: 63: 66: 69] sts.
Work 12 rows.
Row 35 (dec) (RS): As row 21.
Work 13 rows.
Rep last 14 rows twice more, then row 21 (the dec row) again. 49 [52: 55: 58: 61] sts.
Cont straight until 20 rows less have been worked than on back to beg of armhole shaping, ending with RS facing for next row.
Shape front slope
Next row (RS): K to last 4 sts, K2tog tbl, K2.
Working all front slope decreases as set by last row, dec 1 st at front slope edge of every foll 4th row until 44 [47: 50: 53: 56] sts rem.
Work 3 rows, ending with RS facing for next row.
Shape armhole
Cast off 5 [6: 6: 7: 7] sts at beg and dec 1 st at end of next row.
38 [40: 43: 45: 48] sts.
Work 1 row.
Dec 1 st at armhole edge of next 5 [5: 7: 7: 9] rows, then on foll 1 [2: 2: 3: 3] alt rows, then on 2 foll 4th rows **and at same time** dec 1 st at front slope edge on 3rd and every foll 4th row.
26 [27: 27: 28: 28] sts.
Dec 1 st at front slope edge **only** on 4th [2nd: 4th: 2nd: 4th] and every foll 6th [4th: 6th: 4th: 4th] row to 20 [23: 21: 24: 26] sts, then on every foll - [6th: -: 6th: 6th] row until - [20: -: 21: 22] sts rem.
Cont straight until left front matches back to beg of shoulder shaping, ending with RS facing for next row.
Shape shoulder
Cast off 7 sts at beg of next and foll alt row.
Work 1 row.
Cast off rem 6 [6: 7: 7: 8] sts.

RIGHT FRONT

Using 4mm (US 6) needles cast on 46 [49: 52: 55: 58] sts.
Beg with a K row, work in st st as folls:
Work 1 row, ending with **WS** facing for next row.
Inc 1 st at end of next row and at same edge on foll 8 rows, then on foll 2 alt rows, then on foll 4th row. 58 [61: 64: 67: 70] sts.
Work 2 rows, ending with RS facing for next row.
Row 21 (dec) (RS): K to last 24 sts, (K2tog tbl, K10) twice.
Complete to match left front, reversing shapings, working an extra row before beg of armhole and shoulder shaping.

SLEEVES

Using 4mm (US 6) needles cast on 72 [72: 74: 76: 76] sts.
Beg with a K row, work in st st for 16 rows, ending with RS facing for next row.
Row 17 (RS): K7, K2tog, K15, K2tog, K20 [20: 22: 24: 24], K2tog tbl, K15, K2tog tbl, K7.
68 [68: 70: 72: 72] sts.
Work 13 rows.
Row 31: K7, K2tog, K14, K2tog, K18 [18: 20: 22: 22], K2tog tbl, K14, K2tog tbl, K7. 64 [64: 66: 68: 68] sts.
Work 13 rows.
Row 45: K7, K2tog, K13, K2tog, K16 [16: 18: 20: 20], K2tog tbl, K13, K2tog tbl, K7.
60 [60: 62: 64: 64] sts.
Work 13 rows.
Row 59: K7, K2tog, K12, K2tog, K14 [14: 16: 18: 18], K2tog tbl, K12, K2tog tbl, K7.
56 [56: 58: 60: 60] sts.
Work 13 rows.
Row 73: K7, K2tog, K11, K2tog, K12 [12: 14: 16: 16], K2tog tbl, K11, K2tog tbl, K7.
52 [52: 54: 56: 56] sts.
Work 3 rows, ending with RS facing for next row.
Inc 1 st at each end of next and every foll 4th [alt: 4th: 4th: alt] row to 70 [56: 74: 76: 60] sts, then on every foll 6th [4th: 6th: 6th: 4th] row until there are 72 [74: 76: 78: 80] sts.
Cont straight until sleeve meas 43 [43: 44: 44: 44] cm, ending with RS facing for next row.
Shape top
Cast off 5 [6: 6: 7: 7] sts at beg of next 2 rows.
62 [62: 64: 64: 66] sts.

Dec 1 st at each end of next 5 rows, then on foll 2 alt rows, then on every foll 4th row until 36 [36: 38: 38: 40] sts rem.
Work 1 row, ending with RS facing for next row.
Dec 1 st at each end of next and every foll alt row to 28 sts, then on foll 3 rows, ending with RS facing for next row.
Cast off rem 22 sts.

MAKING UP
Press as described on the information page.
See information page for finishing instructions, setting in sleeves using the set-in method.
Edging
Using 4mm (US 6) needles cast on 7 sts.
Knit 1 row.
Cont in patt as folls:
Row 1 (RS): K2, yfwd, sl 1, K1, psso, K1, (yfwd) twice, K1, (yfwd) twice, K1. 11 sts.
Row 2: *K1, (K1, P1) into double yfwd of previous row, rep from * once more, K2, P1, K2.
Row 3: K2, yfwd, sl 1, K1, psso, K7.

Row 4: Cast off 4 sts (one st on right needle), K3, P1, K2. 7 sts.
These 4 rows form patt.
Cont in patt until edging fits around entire hem, front opening and neck edges, ending after patt row 4. Cast off.
Join cast-on and cast-off ends of edging, then sew straight edge in place, positioning edging seam at one side seam.
In same way, make edgings to fit around lower edge of sleeves.
Ties (make 2)
Using double-pointed 3¼mm (US 3) needles cast on 3 sts.
Row 1 (RS): K3, *without turning slip these 3 sts to opposite end of needle and bring yarn to opposite end of work pulling it quite tightly across WS of work, K these 3 sts again, rep from * until tie is 31 cm long, K3tog and fasten off.
Attach one end of each tie to inside of front opening edge, attaching ties to edging seam level with beg of front slope shaping.

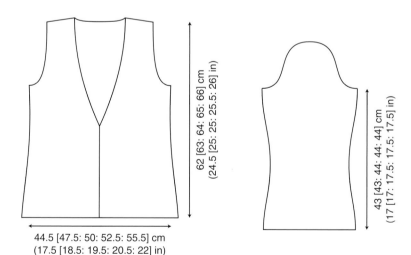

62 [63: 64: 65: 66] cm
(24.5 [25: 25: 25.5: 26] in)

44.5 [47.5: 50: 52.5: 55.5] cm
(17.5 [18.5: 19.5: 20.5: 22] in)

43 [43: 44: 44: 44] cm
(17 [17: 17.5: 17.5: 17.5] in)

Hudson

YARN

	XS	S	M	L	XL	
To fit bust	81	86	91	97	102	cm
	32	34	36	38	40	in

RYC Cashsoft DK

	13	14	14	15	16	x 50gm

(photographed in Bella Donna 502)

NEEDLES

1 pair 3¼mm (no 10) (US 3) needles
1 pair 4mm (no 8) (US 6) needles
Cable needle

TENSION

22 sts and 30 rows to 10 cm measured over
stocking stitch using 4mm (US 6) needles.

SPECIAL ABBREVIATIONS

C6F = slip next 3 sts onto cable needle and leave
at front of work, K3, then K3 from cable needle
C6B = slip next 3 sts onto cable needle and leave
at back of work, K3, then K3 from cable needle
Tw2L = slip next st onto cable needle and leave
at front of work, K1, then K1 from cable needle
Tw2R = slip next st onto cable needle and leave
at back of work, K1, then K1 from cable needle

BACK

Using 3¼mm (US 3) needles cast on 121 [127:
133: 139: 145] sts.
Row 1 (RS): Knit.
Row 2: *P2, K2, P2, rep from * to last st, P1.
Row 3: K1, *K1, Tw2L, K3, rep from * to end.
Row 4: *P2, (K1, P1) twice, rep from * to last st, P1.
Row 5: K1, *K2, Tw2L, K2, rep from * to end.
Row 6: *P3, K2, P1, rep from * to last st, P1.
Row 7: Knit.
Row 8: As row 6.
Row 9: K1, *K2, Tw2R, K2, rep from * to end.
Row 10: As row 4.
Row 11: K1, *K1, Tw2R, K3, rep from * to end.
Row 12: As row 2.
These 12 rows form fancy rib.
Cont in fancy rib for a further 15 rows, ending
with **WS** facing for next row.
Row 28 (WS): Rib 8 [11: 10: 10: 9], M1, *rib 15 [15:
16: 17: 18], M1, rep from * to last 8 [11: 11: 10: 10] sts,
rib to end. 129 [135: 141: 147: 153] sts.

Change to 4mm (US 6) needles.
Beg and ending rows as indicated and rep the
24 row patt rep throughout, cont in patt from
chart for back until back meas 42 [43: 43: 44: 44]
cm, ending with RS facing for next row.
Shape armholes
Keeping patt correct, cast off 5 [6: 6: 7: 7] sts at
beg of next 2 rows. 119 [123: 129: 133: 139] sts.
Dec 1 st at each end of next 7 [7: 9: 9: 11] rows,
then on foll 4 [5: 5: 6: 6] alt rows, then on every
foll 4th row until 93 [95: 97: 99: 101] sts rem.
Cont straight until armhole meas 23 [23: 24: 24:
25] cm, ending with RS facing for next row.
Shape shoulders and back neck
Cast off 7 [7: 8: 8: 8] sts at beg of next 2 rows.
79 [81: 81: 83: 85] sts.
Next row (RS): Cast off 7 [7: 8: 8: 8] sts, patt until
there are 12 [12: 11: 11: 12] sts on right needle and
turn, leaving rem sts on a holder.
Work each side of neck separately.
Cast off 4 sts at beg of next row.
Cast off rem 8 [8: 7: 7: 8] sts.
With RS facing, rejoin yarn to rem sts, cast off
centre 41 [43: 43: 45: 45] sts dec 6 sts evenly,
patt to end.
Complete to match first side, reversing shapings.

FRONT

Work as given for back until 18 [18: 18: 20: 20]
rows less have been worked than on back to beg
of shoulder shaping, ending with RS facing for
next row.
Shape neck
Next row (RS): Patt 33 [33: 34: 35: 36] sts and
turn, leaving rem sts on a holder.
Work each side of neck separately.
Dec 1 st at neck edge on next 7 rows, then on foll
3 [3: 3: 4: 4] alt rows, then on foll 4th row, ending
with RS facing for next row.
22 [22: 23: 23: 24] sts.
Shape shoulder
Cast off 7 [7: 8: 8: 8] sts at beg of next and foll
alt row.
Work 1 row.
Cast off rem 8 [8: 7: 7: 8] sts.
With RS facing, rejoin yarn to rem sts, cast off
centre 27 [29: 29: 29: 29] sts dec 6 sts evenly,
patt to end.

Complete to match first side, reversing shapings,
working an extra row before beg of shoulder
shaping.

SLEEVES

Using 3¼mm (US 3) needles cast on 61 sts.
Work in fancy rib as given for back for 27 rows,
ending with **WS** facing for next row.
Row 28 (WS): Rib 20 [20: 6: 5: 5], M1, (rib 21 [21:
16: 10: 10], M1) 1 [1: 3: 5: 5] times, rib to end.
63 [63: 65: 67: 67] sts.
Change to 4mm (US 6) needles.
Beg and ending rows as indicated and rep the
24 row patt rep throughout, cont in patt from chart
for sleeves, shaping sides by inc 1 st at each end
of 7th [5th: 5th: 5th: 5th] and every foll 8th [6th:
8th: 8th: 6th] row until there are 83 [67: 91: 93:
77] sts, then on every foll 10th [8th: -: -: 8th] row
until there are 87 [89: -: -: 95] sts, taking inc sts
into moss st.
Cont straight until sleeve meas 46 [46: 47: 47:
47] cm, ending with RS facing for next row.
Shape top
Keeping patt correct, cast off 5 [6: 6: 7: 7] sts at
beg of next 2 rows. 77 [77: 79: 79: 81] sts.
Dec 1 st at each end of next 7 rows, then on foll
5 alt rows, then on every foll 4th row until 45 [45:
47: 47: 49] sts rem.
Work 1 row, ending with RS facing for next row.
Dec 1 st at each end of next and every foll alt row
to 35 sts, then on foll row, ending with RS facing
for next row. 33 sts.
Cast off 5 sts at beg of next 2 rows.
Cast off rem 23 sts.

MAKING UP

Press as described on the information page.
Join right shoulder seam using back stitch, or
mattress stitch if preferred.
Neckband
With RS facing and using 3¼mm (US 3) needles,
pick up and knit 21 [22: 22: 24: 24] sts down left
side of neck, 24 [26: 26: 26: 26] sts from front,
21 [22: 22: 24: 24] sts up right side of neck, then
43 [45: 45: 47: 47] sts from back.
109 [115: 115: 121: 121] sts.
Beg with row 2, work in fancy rib as given for back
for 17 rows, ending with RS facing for next row.

Cast off in rib.
See information page for finishing instructions,
setting in sleeves using the set-in method.

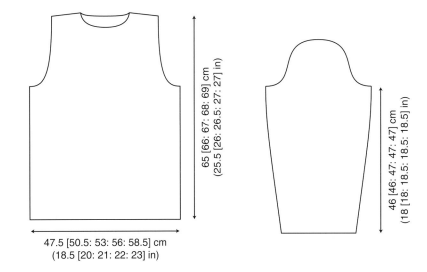

65 [66: 67: 68: 69] cm
(25.5 [26: 26.5: 27: 27] in)

46 [46: 47: 47: 47] cm
(18 [18: 18.5: 18.5: 18.5] in)

47.5 [50.5: 53: 56: 58.5] cm
(18.5 [20: 21: 22: 23] in)

Back chart

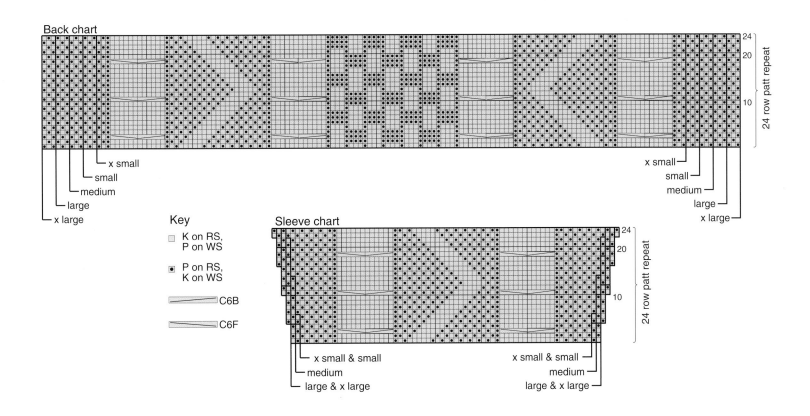

24
20
10

24 row patt repeat

x small
small
medium
large
x large

x small
small
medium
large
x large

Key

▫ K on RS,
P on WS

▪ P on RS,
K on WS

▱ C6B

▱ C6F

Sleeve chart

24
20
10

24 row patt repeat

x small & small
medium
large & x large

x small & small
medium
large & x large

Jersey

YARN

		XS	S	M	L	XL	
To fit bust		81	86	91	97	102	cm
		32	34	36	38	40	in

RYC Cashsoft DK

A	Mirage	503	3	4	4	4	4	x 50gm
B	Poppy	512	5	6	6	6	7	x 50gm

NEEDLES

1 pair 3¼mm (no 10) (US 3) needles
1 pair 4mm (no 8) (US 6) needles

TENSION

22 sts and 30 rows to 10 cm measured over
stocking stitch using 4mm (US 6) needles.

BACK

Using 3¼mm (US 3) needles and yarn A cast on
95 [101: 107: 113: 119] sts.
Work in g st for 5 rows, ending with **WS** facing for
next row.
Row 6 (WS): K5 and slip these sts onto a holder,
K to last 5 sts and turn, leaving rem 5 sts on
another holder. 85 [91: 97: 103: 109] sts.
Change to 4mm (US 6) needles.
Join in yarn B and, beg with a K row, cont in
striped st st as folls:
Using yarn B, work 4 rows.
Using yarn A, work 2 rows.
These 6 rows form striped st st.
Cont in striped st st for a further 20 rows, ending
with RS facing for next row.
Keeping stripes correct, cast on 5 sts at beg of
next 2 rows. 95 [101: 107: 113: 119] sts.
Dec 1 st at each end of 3rd and every foll 4th row
until 83 [89: 95: 101: 107] sts rem.
Work 9 rows, ending with RS facing for next row.
Inc 1 st at each end of next and every foll 6th row
until there are 95 [101: 107: 113: 119] sts.
Cont straight until back meas 35 [36: 36: 37: 37] cm,
ending with RS facing for next row.
Shape armholes
Keeping stripes correct, cast off 4 [5: 5: 6: 6] sts
at beg of next 2 rows.
87 [91: 97: 101: 107] sts.
Dec 1 st at each end of next 3 [3: 5: 5: 7] rows,
then on foll 2 [3: 3: 4: 4] alt rows, then on every
foll 4th row until 73 [75: 77: 79: 81] sts rem.

Cont straight until armhole meas 20 [20: 21:
21: 22] cm, ending with RS facing for next row.
Shape shoulders and back neck
Cast off 4 [4: 4: 4: 5] sts at beg of next 2 rows.
65 [67: 69: 71: 71] sts.
Next row (RS): Cast off 4 [4: 4: 4: 5] sts, K until
there are 8 [8: 9: 9: 8] sts on right needle and
turn, leaving rem sts on a holder.
Work each side of neck separately.
Cast off 4 sts at beg of next row.
Cast off rem 4 [4: 5: 5: 4] sts.
With RS facing, rejoin yarns to rem sts, cast off
centre 41 [43: 43: 45: 45] sts, K to end.
Complete to match first side, reversing shapings.

FRONT

Work as given for back until 12 [12: 12: 14: 14]
rows less have been worked than on back to beg
of shoulder shaping, ending with RS facing for
next row.
Shape neck
Next row (RS): K20 [20: 21: 22: 23] and turn,
leaving rem sts on a holder.
Work each side of neck separately.
Dec 1 st at neck edge on next 5 rows, then on foll
3 [3: 3: 4: 4] alt rows, ending with RS facing for
next row. 12 [12: 13: 13: 14] sts.
Shape shoulder
Cast off 4 [4: 4: 4: 5] sts at beg of next and foll alt
row.
Work 1 row.
Cast off rem 4 [4: 5: 5: 4] sts.
With RS facing, rejoin yarn to rem sts, cast off
centre 33 [35: 35: 35: 35] sts, K to end.
Complete to match first side, reversing shapings,
working an extra row before beg of shoulder
shaping.

SLEEVES

Using 3¼mm (US 3) needles and yarn A cast on
55 [55: 57: 59: 59] sts.
Work in g st for 6 rows, ending with RS facing for
next row.
Change to 4mm (US 6) needles.
Join in yarn B and, beg with a K row, cont in
striped st st as given for back, shaping sides by
inc 1 st at each end of next and every foll 10th
[8th: 8th: 8th: 8th] row to 69 [63: 63: 65: 75] sts,

then on every foll 12th [10th: 10th: 10th: 10th] row
until there are 73 [75: 77: 79: 81] sts.
Cont straight until sleeve meas 34 [34: 35:
35: 35] cm, ending after same stripe row as on
back to beg of armhole shaping and with RS
facing for next row.
Shape top
Keeping stripes correct, cast off 4 [5: 5: 6: 6] sts
at beg of next 2 rows. 65 [65: 67: 67: 69] sts.
Dec 1 st at each end of next 3 rows, then on foll
3 alt rows, then on every foll 4th row until 43 [43:
45: 45: 47] sts rem.
Work 1 row, ending with RS facing for next row.
Dec 1 st at each end of next and every foll alt row
to 33 sts, then on foll 5 rows, ending with
RS facing for next row.
Cast off rem 23 sts.

MAKING UP

Press as described on the information page.
Join right shoulder seam using back stitch, or
mattress stitch if preferred.
Neckband
With RS facing, using 3¼mm (US 3) needles and
yarn A, pick up and knit 15 [15: 15: 17: 17] sts down
left side of neck, 33 [35: 35: 35: 35] sts from front,
15 [15: 15: 17: 17] sts up right side of neck, then
49 [51: 51: 53: 53] sts from back.
112 [116: 116: 122: 122] sts.
Beg with a K row, work in rev st st for 4 rows.
Cast off knitwise (on **WS**).
**Right front and left back side opening borders
(both alike)**
Slip 5 sts left on holder onto 3¼mm (US 3) needles
and rejoin yarn A with RS facing.
Cont in g st until border, when slightly stretched,
fits up row-end edge to cast-on sts, ending with
WS facing for next row.
Cast off.
**Left front and right back side opening borders
(both alike)**
Work to match right front and left back side
opening borders, rejoining yarn with **WS** facing.
Slip st borders in place to row-end and cast-on
edges.
See information page for finishing instructions,
setting in sleeves using the set-in method,
leaving side seams open along edges of borders.

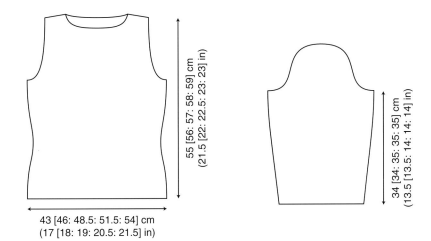

55 [56: 57: 58: 59] cm
(21.5 [22: 22.5: 23: 23] in)

43 [46: 48.5: 51.5: 54] cm
(17 [18: 19: 20.5: 21.5] in)

34 [34: 35: 35: 35] cm
(13.5 [13.5: 14: 14: 14] in)

Madison

YARN

	XS	S	M	L	XL	
To fit bust	81	86	91	97	102	cm
	32	34	36	38	40	in

RYC Cashsoft DK

			XS	S	M	L	XL	
A	Cream	500	4	4	4	5	5	x 50gm
B	Ballad Blue	508	4	4	4	5	5	x 50gm
C	Black	519	4	4	4	5	5	x 50gm

NEEDLES

1 pair 3¼mm (no 10) (US 3) needles
1 pair 4mm (no 8) (US 6) needles

BUTTONS – 7 x 75339

TENSION

22 sts and 32 rows to 10 cm measured over pattern using 4mm (US 6) needles.

BACK

Using 3¼mm (US 3) needles and yarn A cast on 95 [101: 107: 113: 119] sts.
Beg with a K row, work in st st for 7 rows, ending with **WS** facing for next row.
Row 8 (WS): Knit (to form fold line).
Change to 4mm (US 6) needles.
Joining in and breaking off colours as required, cont in patt as folls:
Row 1 (RS): Using yarn A, purl.
Row 2: Using yarn A, knit.
Rows 3 and 4: Using yarn B, knit.
Row 5: Using yarn B, purl.
Row 6: Using yarn C, knit.
Row 7: Using yarn C, purl.
Row 8: Using yarn C, knit.
Rows 9 and 10: Using yarn A, knit.
Row 11: Using yarn A, purl.
Row 12: Using yarn B, knit.
Row 13: Using yarn B, purl.
Row 14: Using yarn B, knit.
Rows 15 and 16: Using yarn C, knit.
Row 17: Using yarn C, purl.
Row 18: Using yarn A, knit.
These 18 rows form patt.
Cont in patt, shaping side seams by dec 1 st at each end of 7th and every foll 8th row to 89 [95: 101: 107: 113] sts, then on every foll 6th row to 85 [91: 97: 103: 109] sts, then on every foll 4th row until 81 [87: 93: 99: 105] sts rem.

Work 11 rows, ending with RS facing for next row.
Inc 1 st at each end of next and every foll 6th row until there are 95 [101: 107: 113: 119] sts.
Cont straight until back meas 38 [39: 39: 40: 40] cm **from fold line row**, ending with RS facing for next row.

Shape armholes

Keeping patt correct, cast off 4 [5: 5: 6: 6] sts at beg of next 2 rows. 87 [91: 97: 101: 107] sts.
Dec 1 st at each end of next 3 [3: 5: 5: 7] rows, then on foll 2 [3: 3: 4: 4] alt rows, then on every foll 4th row until 73 [75: 77: 79: 81] sts rem.
Cont straight until armhole meas 20 [20: 21: 21: 22] cm, ending with RS facing for next row.

Shape shoulders and back neck

Cast off 7 [7: 7: 7: 8] sts at beg of next 2 rows.
59 [61: 63: 65: 65] sts.
Next row (RS): Cast off 7 [7: 7: 7: 8] sts, patt until there are 11 [11: 12: 12: 11] sts on right needle and turn, leaving rem sts on a holder.
Work each side of neck separately.
Cast off 4 sts at beg of next row.
Cast off rem 7 [7: 8: 8: 7] sts.
With RS facing, rejoin yarns to rem sts, cast off centre 23 [25: 25: 27: 27] sts, patt to end.
Complete to match first side, reversing shapings.

LEFT FRONT

Using 3¼mm (US 3) needles and yarn A cast on 48 [51: 54: 57: 60] sts.
Beg with a K row, work in st st for 7 rows, ending with **WS** facing for next row.
Row 8 (WS): Knit (to form fold line).
Change to 4mm (US 6) needles.
Cont in patt as given for back, shaping side seam by dec 1 st at beg of 7th and every foll 8th row to 45 [48: 51: 54: 57] sts, then on every foll 6th row to 43 [46: 49: 52: 55] sts, then on every foll 4th row until 41 [44: 47: 50: 53] sts rem.
Work 11 rows, ending with RS facing for next row.
Inc 1 st at beg of next and every foll 6th row until there are 48 [51: 54: 57: 60] sts.
Cont straight until left front matches back to beg of armhole shaping, ending with RS facing for next row.

Shape armhole

Keeping patt correct, cast off 4 [5: 5: 6: 6] sts at beg of next row. 44 [46: 49: 51: 54] sts.

Work 1 row.
Dec 1 st at armhole edge of next 3 [3: 5: 5: 7] rows, then on foll 2 [3: 3: 4: 4] alt rows, then on every foll 4th row until 37 [38: 39: 40: 41] sts rem.
Cont straight until 17 [17: 17: 19: 19] rows less have been worked than on back to beg of shoulder shaping, ending with **WS** facing for next row.

Shape neck

Keeping patt correct, cast off 8 [9: 9: 9: 9] sts at beg of next row.
29 [29: 30: 31: 32] sts.
Dec 1 st at neck edge on next 4 rows, then on foll 2 [2: 2: 3: 3] alt rows, then on every foll 4th row until 21 [21: 22: 22: 23] sts rem, ending with RS facing for next row.

Shape shoulder

Cast off 7 [7: 7: 7: 8] sts at beg of next and foll alt row.
Work 1 row.
Cast off rem 7 [7: 8: 8: 7] sts.

RIGHT FRONT

Using 3¼mm (US 3) needles and yarn A cast on 48 [51: 54: 57: 60] sts.
Beg with a K row, work in st st for 7 rows, ending with **WS** facing for next row.
Row 8 (WS): Knit (to form fold line).
Change to 4mm (US 6) needles.
Cont in patt as given for back, shaping side seam by dec 1 st at end of 7th and every foll 8th row to 45 [48: 51: 54: 57] sts, then on every foll 6th row to 43 [46: 49: 52: 55] sts, then on every foll 4th row until 41 [44: 47: 50: 53] sts rem.
Complete to match left front, reversing shapings, working an extra row before beg of armhole, neck and shoulder shaping.

SLEEVES

Using 3¼mm (US 3) needles and yarn A cast on 51 [51: 53: 55: 55] sts.
Beg with a K row, work in st st for 7 rows, ending with **WS** facing for next row.
Row 8 (WS): Knit (to form fold line).
Change to 4mm (US 6) needles.
Cont in patt as given for back, shaping sides by inc 1 st at each end of 9th [9th: 9th: 9th: 7th] and every foll 10th row to 61 [71: 73: 71: 81] sts, then

on every foll 12th [12th: 12th: 12th: -] row until
there are 73 [75: 77: 79: -] sts.

Cont straight until sleeve meas approx 43 [44:
44: 45: 45] cm **from fold line row**, ending after
same patt row as on back to beg of armhole
shaping and with RS facing for next row.

Shape top

Keeping patt correct, cast off 4 [5: 5: 6: 6] sts at
beg of next 2 rows.

65 [65: 67: 67: 69] sts.

Dec 1 st at each end of next 3 rows, then on foll
3 alt rows, then on every foll 4th row until
39 [39: 41: 41: 43] sts rem.

Work 1 row, ending with RS facing for next row.

Dec 1 st at each end of next and every foll
alt row to 33 sts, then on foll 5 rows,
ending with RS facing for next row.

Cast off rem 23 sts.

MAKING UP

Press as described on the information page.
Join both shoulder seams using back stitch, or
mattress stitch if preferred.

Collar

With RS facing, using 3¼mm (US 3) needles and
yarn A, starting and ending at front opening
edges, pick up and knit 29 [30: 30: 32: 32] sts up
right side of neck, 31 [33: 33: 35: 35] sts from
back, then 29 [30: 30: 32: 32] sts down left side
of neck.

89 [93: 93: 99: 99] sts.

Knit 1 row, ending with WS of collar (RS of body)
facing for next row.

Beg with row 1, work in patt as given for back
for 32 rows, ending with WS of collar facing for
next row.

Break off yarns A and B and cont using yarn C
only.

Work in g st for 5 rows, ending with RS of collar
facing for next row.

Cast off knitwise.

Buttonhole band

With RS of collar (WS of body) facing, using
3¼mm (US 3) needles and yarn B, pick up and
knit 23 sts down right front end of collar, beg at
cast-off edge.

Break yarn and set sts to one side.

With RS of body facing, using 3¼mm (US 3)
needles and yarn B, beg at fold line row, pick up
and knit 121 [123: 125: 125: 127] sts up right front
opening edge to collar pick-up row, then K across
23 sts picked up along end of collar.

144 [146: 148: 148: 150] sts.

Work in g st for 4 rows, ending with **WS** of body
facing for next row.

Row 5 (WS): K26 [28: 29: 29: 31], *cast off 2 sts,
K until there are 17 sts on right needle after cast-
off, rep from * 5 times more, cast off 2 sts, K to end.
Break off yarn B and join in yarn C.

Row 6: K to end, casting on 2 sts over those cast
off on previous row.

Work in g st for a further 4 rows, ending with **WS**
of body facing for next row.

Cast off knitwise (on **WS**).

Button band

With RS of collar (WS of body) facing, using
3¼mm (US 3) needles and yarn B, pick up and
knit 23 sts up left front end of collar, beg at collar
pick-up row, turn and K these 23 sts, then with
RS of body facing, pick up and knit 121 [123: 125:
125: 127] sts down left front opening edge to fold
line row. 144 [146: 148: 148: 150] sts.

Work in g st for 5 rows, ending with RS of body
facing for next row.

Break off yarn B and join in yarn C.

Work in g st for 5 rows, ending with **WS** of body
facing for next row.

Cast off knitwise (on **WS**).

See information page for finishing instructions,
setting in sleeves using the set-in method. Fold
first 7 rows to inside along fold line row around
lower edge of body and sleeves and stitch in place.

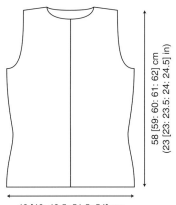

58 [59: 60: 61: 62] cm
(23 [23: 23.5: 24: 24.5] in)

43 [46: 48.5: 51.5: 54] cm
(17 [18: 19: 20.5: 21.5] in)

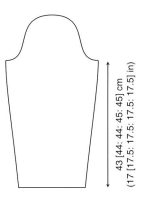

43 [44: 44: 45: 45] cm
(17 [17.5: 17.5: 17.5: 17.5] in)

YARN

	XS	S	M	L	XL	
To fit bust	81	86	91	97	102	cm
	32	34	36	38	40	in

RYC Cashsoft DK

| | 13 | 14 | 15 | 15 | 16 | x 50gm |

(photographed in Bella Donna 502)

NEEDLES

1 pair 3mm (no 11) (US 2/3) needles
1 pair 3¾mm (no 9) (US 5) needles
3.50mm (no 9) (US E4) crochet hook

BUTTONS – 6 x 75319

TENSION

24 sts and 35 rows to 10 cm measured over moss stitch using 3¾mm (US 5) needles.

CROCHET ABBREVIATIONS

dc=double crochet; **ch**=chain; **ss**=slip stitch.

BACK

Using 3mm (US 2/3) needles cast on 105 [111: 117: 123: 129] sts.
Row 1 (RS): K1, *P1, K1, rep from * to end.
Row 2: As row 1.
These 2 rows form moss st.
Work in moss st for a further 6 rows, ending with RS facing for next row.
Change to 3¾mm (US 5) needles.
Cont in moss st, shaping side seams by dec 1 st at each end of 15th and every foll 8th row to 97 [103: 109: 115: 121] sts, then on every foll 6th row until 91 [97: 103: 109: 115] sts rem.
Work 11 rows, ending with RS facing for next row.
Inc 1 st at each end of next and every foll 6th row until there are 105 [111: 117: 123: 129] sts.
Cont straight until back meas 35 [36: 36: 37: 37] cm, ending with RS facing for next row.
Shape armholes
Keeping moss st correct, cast off 5 [6: 6: 7: 7] sts at beg of next 2 rows. 95 [99: 105: 109: 115] sts.
Dec 1 st at each end of next 5 [5: 7: 7: 9] rows, then on foll 1 [2: 2: 3: 3] alt rows, then on every foll 4th row until 79 [81: 83: 85: 87] sts rem.
Cont straight until armhole meas 20 [20: 21: 21: 22] cm, ending with RS facing for next row.

Shape shoulders and back neck
Cast off 7 [7: 8: 8: 8] sts at beg of next 2 rows. 65 [67: 67: 69: 71] sts.
Next row (RS): Cast off 7 [7: 8: 8: 8] sts, moss st until there are 12 [12: 11: 11: 12] sts on right needle and turn, leaving rem sts on a holder.
Work each side of neck separately.
Cast off 4 sts at beg of next row.
Cast off rem 8 [8: 7: 7: 8] sts.
With RS facing, rejoin yarn to rem sts, cast off centre 27 [29: 29: 31: 31] sts, moss st to end.
Complete to match first side, reversing shapings.

LEFT FRONT
Using 3mm (US 2/3) needles cast on 60 [63: 66: 69: 72] sts.
Row 1 (RS): *K1, P1, rep from * to last 0 [1: 0: 1: 0] st, K0 [1: 0: 1: 0].
Row 2: K0 [1: 0: 1: 0], *P1, K1, rep from * to end.
These 2 rows form moss st.
Work in moss st for a further 5 rows, ending with **WS** facing for next row.
Row 8 (WS): Moss st 7 sts and slip these sts onto a holder, moss st to end.
53 [56: 59: 62: 65] sts.
Change to 3¾ (US 5) needles.
Cont in moss st, shaping side seam by dec 1 st at beg of 15th and every foll 8th row to 49 [52: 55: 58: 61] sts, then on every foll 6th row until 46 [49: 52: 55: 58] sts rem.
Work 11 rows, ending with RS facing for next row.
Inc 1 st at beg of next and every foll 6th row until there are 53 [56: 59: 62: 65] sts.
Cont straight until 6 rows less have been worked than on back to beg of armhole shaping, ending with RS facing for next row.
Shape front slope
Dec 1 st at end of next and foll 1 [2: 1: 2: 1] alt rows.
51 [53: 57: 59: 63] sts.
Work 3 [1: 3: 1: 3] rows, ending with RS facing for next row.
Shape armhole
Cast off 5 [6: 6: 7: 7] sts at beg and dec 1 st at end of next row. 45 [46: 50: 51: 55] sts.
Work 1 row.
Dec 1 st at armhole edge of next 5 [5: 7: 7: 9] rows, then on foll 1 [2: 2: 3: 3] alt rows,

then on 2 foll 4th rows **and at same time** dec 1 st at front slope edge on 3rd and every foll 4th row. 33 [33: 34: 34: 35] sts.
Dec 1 st at front slope edge **only** on 4th [2nd: 4th: 2nd: 4th] and every foll 4th row until 22 [22: 23: 23: 24] sts rem.
Cont straight until left front matches back to beg of shoulder shaping, ending with RS facing for next row.
Shape shoulder
Cast off 7 [7: 8: 8: 8] sts at beg of next and foll alt row.
Work 1 row.
Cast off rem 8 [8: 7: 7: 8] sts.

RIGHT FRONT
Using 3mm (US 2/3) needles cast on 60 [63: 66: 69: 72] sts.
Row 1 (RS): K0 [1: 0: 1: 0], *P1, K1, rep from * to end.
Row 2: *K1, P1, rep from * to last 0 [1: 0: 1: 0] st, K0 [1: 0: 1: 0].
These 2 rows form moss st.
Work in moss st for a further 2 rows, ending with RS facing for next row.
Row 5 (RS): Moss st 2 sts, work 2 tog, yrn (to make a buttonhole), moss st to end.
Work in moss st for a further 2 rows, ending with **WS** facing for next row.
Row 8 (WS): Moss st to last 7 sts and turn, leaving rem 7 sts on a holder. 53 [56: 59: 62: 65] sts.
Change to 3¾mm (US 5) needles.
Cont in moss st, shaping side seam by dec 1 st at end of 15th and every foll 8th row to 49 [52: 55: 58: 61] sts, then on every foll 6th row until 46 [49: 52: 55: 58] sts rem.
Complete to match left front, reversing shapings, working an extra row before beg of armhole and shoulder shaping.

SLEEVES
Using 3mm (US 2/3) needles cast on 77 [77: 79: 81: 81] sts.
Work in moss st as given for back for 8 rows, ending with RS facing for next row.
Change to 3¾mm (US 5) needles.
Cont in moss st, dec 1 st at each end of next and every foll 8th row to 69 [69: 71: 73: 73] sts, then on foll 6th row. 67 [67: 69: 71: 71] sts.

Work 5 rows, ending with RS facing for next row.
Inc 1 st at each end of next row.
69 [69: 71: 73: 73] sts.
Place markers at both ends of last row.
Work 5 rows, ending with RS facing for next row.
Dec 1 st at each end of next and every foll 8th row
until 57 [57: 59: 61: 61] sts rem.
Work 7 rows, ending with RS facing for next row.
Inc 1 st at each end of next and every foll alt row
to 61 [65: 63: 65: 69] sts, then on every foll
4th row until there are 79 [81: 83: 85: 87] sts.
Cont straight until sleeve meas 43 [43: 44:
44: 44] cm, ending with RS facing for next row.

Shape top
Cast off 5 [6: 6: 7: 7] sts at beg of next 2 rows.
69 [69: 71: 71: 73] sts.
Dec 1 st at each end of next 5 rows, then on foll
2 alt rows, then on every foll 4th row until
43 [43: 45: 45: 47] sts rem.
Work 1 row, ending with RS facing for next row.
Dec 1 st at each end of next and every foll alt row
to 31 sts, then on foll 5 rows, ending with RS
facing for next row.
Cast off rem 21 sts.

MAKING UP
Press as described on the information page.
Join both shoulder seams using back stitch, or
mattress stitch if preferred.
Place markers along front slopes 9 cm below
shoulder seams.

Button band and left collar
Slip 7 sts from left front holder onto 3mm (US 2/3)
needles and rejoin yarn with RS facing.
Cont in moss st as set until band, when slightly
stretched, fits up left front opening edge to beg
of front slope shaping, ending with RS facing for
next row.

Shape for collar
Next row (RS of body, WS of collar): Moss st 1 st,
inc twice in next st, moss st to end.
Work 5 rows.
Rep last 6 rows until there are 21 sts.
Cont straight until collar, unstretched, fits up left
front slope to marker, ending with RS of collar
facing for next row.

Next row (RS of collar): Cast off 9 sts, turn, cast
on and moss st 9 sts, moss st to end.
Cont straight until collar, unstretched, fits up left
front slope and across to centre back neck.
Cast off in moss st.
Slip st band and collar in place.
Mark positions for 6 buttons on this band – first
to come level with buttonhole already worked in
right front, last to come 1 cm below beg of front
slope shaping, and rem 4 buttons evenly spaced
between.

Buttonhole band and right collar
Slip 7 sts from right front holder onto 3mm (US 2/3)
needles and rejoin yarn with **WS** facing.
Cont in moss st as set until band, when slightly
stretched, fits up right front opening edge to beg
of front slope shaping, ending with RS facing for
next row and with the addition of a further
5 buttonholes worked to correspond with
positions marked for buttons as folls:
Next row (buttonhole row) (RS): Moss st 2 sts, work
2 tog, yrn (to make a buttonhole), moss st 3 sts.

Shape for collar
Next row (RS of body, WS of collar): moss st to
last 2 sts, inc twice in next st, moss st 1 st.
Complete to match button band and left collar,
reversing shapings.
Slip st band and collar in place, joining ends of
collar at centre back neck.
See information page for finishing instructions,
setting in sleeves using the set-in method and
leaving sleeve seams open below markers.

Crochet edging
Using 3.50mm (US E4) crochet hook and with
RS facing, attach yarn at base of one side seam
and work one round of dc evenly around entire
hem, front opening and collar edges, working
3 dc into each corner point and ending with
ss to first dc.
Next round (RS): 1 ch (does NOT count as st),
1 dc into first dc, *28 ch, 1 dc into next dc,
rep from * to end, 28 ch, ss to first dc.
Fasten off.
In same way, starting and ending at top of sleeve
opening, work edging around lower edge of sleeves.

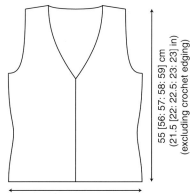

55 [56: 57: 58: 59] cm
(21.5 [22: 22.5: 23: 23] in)
(excluding crochet edging)

44 [46.5: 49: 51.5: 54] cm
(17.5 [18.5: 19.5: 20.5: 21.5] in)

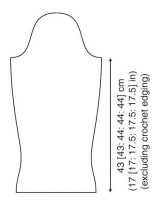

43 [43: 44: 44: 44] cm
(17 [17: 17.5: 17.5: 17.5] in)
(excluding crochet edging)

Plaza

YARN

	XS	S	M	L	XL	
To fit bust	81	86	91	97	102	cm
	32	34	36	38	40	in

RYC Cashcotton DK

	9	9	10	10	11	x 50gm

(photographed in Apple 603)

NEEDLES
1 pair 3¼mm (no 10) (US 3) needles
1 pair 4mm (no 8) (US 6) needles
3.50mm (no 9) (US E4) crochet hook

BUTTONS - 5

TENSION
22 sts and 30 rows to 10 cm measured over stocking stitch using 4mm (US 6) needles.

CROCHET ABBREVIATIONS
dc=double crochet; **ch**=chain; **tr**=treble;
dc2tog=(insert hook into next st, yarn over hook and draw loop through) twice, yarn over hook and draw through all 3 loops on hook.

BACK
Using 3¼mm (US 3) needles cast on 95 [101: 107: 113: 119] sts.
Work in g st for 12 rows, ending with RS facing for next row.
Change to 4mm (US 6) needles.
Beg with a K row, cont in st st, shaping side seams by dec 1 st at each end of 3rd and every foll 6th row to 89 [95: 101: 107: 113] sts, then on every foll 4th row until 83 [89: 95: 101: 107] sts rem.
Cont straight until back meas 14 [15: 15: 16: 16] cm, ending with RS facing for next row.
Inc 1 st at each end of next and every foll 8th row until there are 95 [101: 107: 113: 119] sts.
Work 7 rows, ending with RS facing for next row.
(Back should meas 30 [31: 31: 32: 32] cm.)
Shape armholes
Cast off 5 [6: 6: 7: 7] sts at beg of next 2 rows.
85 [89: 95: 99: 105] sts.
Dec 1 st at each end of next 3 [3: 5: 5: 7] rows, then on foll 2 [3: 3: 4: 4] alt rows, then on foll 4th row.
73 [75: 77: 79: 81] sts.

Cont straight until armhole meas 20 [20: 21: 21: 22] cm, ending with RS facing for next row.
Shape shoulders and back neck
Cast off 7 [7: 7: 7: 8] sts at beg of next 2 rows.
59 [61: 63: 65: 65] sts.
Next row (RS): Cast off 7 [7: 7: 7: 8] sts, K until there are 11 [11: 12: 12: 11] sts on right needle and turn, leaving rem sts on a holder.
Work each side of neck separately.
Cast off 4 sts at beg of next row.
Cast off rem 7 [7: 8: 8: 7] sts.
With RS facing, rejoin yarn to rem sts, cast off centre 23 [25: 25: 27: 27] sts, K to end.
Complete to match first side, reversing shapings.

LEFT FRONT
Using 3¼mm (US 3) needles cast on 56 [59: 62: 65: 68] sts.
Work in g st for 11 rows, ending with **WS** facing for next row.
Row 12 (WS): K8 and slip these sts onto a holder, K to end. 48 [51: 54: 57: 60] sts.
Change to 4mm (US 6) needles.
Beg with a K row, cont in st st, shaping side seam by dec 1 st at beg of 3rd and every foll 6th row to 45 [48: 51: 54: 57] sts, then on every foll 4th row until 42 [45: 48: 51: 54] sts rem.
Cont straight until left front meas 14 [15: 15: 16: 16] cm, ending with RS facing for next row.
Inc 1 st at beg of next and every foll 8th row until there are 46 [49: 52: 55: 58] sts.
Work 3 rows, ending with RS facing for next row.
Shape front slope
Dec 1 st at end of next and 4 foll 4th rows and at same time inc 1 st at beg of 5th and foll 8th row.
43 [46: 49: 52: 55] sts.
Work 3 rows, ending with RS facing for next row.
(Left front should now match back to beg of armhole shaping.)
Shape armhole
Cast off 5 [6: 6: 7: 7] sts at beg and dec 1 st at end of next row. 37 [39: 42: 44: 47] sts.
Work 1 row.
Dec 1 st at armhole edge of next 3 [3: 5: 5: 7] rows, then on foll 2 [3: 3: 4: 4] alt rows, then on foll 4th row **and at same time** dec 1 st at front slope edge on 3rd and every foll 4th row.
28 [29: 29: 30: 30] sts.

Dec 1 st at front slope edge **only** on 4th [2nd: 4th: 2nd: 4th] and every foll 4th row to 26 [24: 27: 25: 27] sts, then on every foll 6th row until 21 [21: 22: 22: 23] sts rem.
Cont straight until left front matches back to beg of shoulder shaping, ending with RS facing for next row.
Shape shoulder
Cast off 7 [7: 7: 7: 8] sts at beg of next and foll alt row.
Work 1 row.
Cast off rem 7 [7: 8: 8: 7] sts.

RIGHT FRONT
Using 3¼mm (US 3) needles cast on 56 [59: 62: 65: 68] sts.
Work in g st for 6 rows, ending with RS facing for next row.
Row 7 (RS): K3, K2tog, yfwd (to make a buttonhole), K to end.
Work in g st for a further 4 rows, ending with **WS** facing for next row.
Row 12 (WS): K to last 8 sts and turn, leaving rem 8 sts on a holder.
48 [51: 54: 57: 60] sts.
Change to 4mm (US 6) needles.
Beg with a K row, cont in st st, shaping side seam by dec 1 st at end of 3rd and every foll 6th row to 45 [48: 51: 54: 57] sts, then on every foll 4th row until 42 [45: 48: 51: 54] sts rem.
Complete to match left front, reversing shapings, working an extra row before beg of armhole and shoulder shaping.

SLEEVES
Using 3¼mm (US 3) needles cast on 61 [61: 63: 65: 65] sts.
Work in g st for 7 cm, ending with RS facing for next row.
Change to 4mm (US 6) needles.
Beg with a K row, cont in st st, shaping sides by inc 1 st at each end of next and every foll 18th [16th: 16th: 16th: 14th] row to 67 [75: 73: 75: 79] sts, then on every foll 20th [-: 18th: 18th: 16th] row until there are 73 [-: 77: 79: 81] sts.
Cont straight until sleeve meas 44 [44: 45: 45: 45] cm, ending with RS facing for next row.

Shape top

Cast off 5 [6: 6: 7: 7] sts at beg of next 2 rows. 63 [63: 65: 65: 67] sts.

Dec 1 st at each end of next 3 rows, then on foll 3 alt rows, then on every foll 4th row until 39 [39: 41: 41: 43] sts rem.

Work 1 row, ending with RS facing for next row.

Dec 1 st at each end of next and every foll alt row to 33 sts, then on foll 5 rows, ending with RS facing for next row.

Cast off rem 23 sts.

MAKING UP

Press as described on the information page.

Join both shoulder seams using back stitch, or mattress stitch if preferred.

Button band and left collar

Slip 8 sts from left front holder onto 3¼mm (US 3) needles and rejoin yarn with RS facing.

Cont in g st until band, when slightly stretched, fits up left front opening edge to beg of front slope shaping, ending with RS facing for next row.

Shape for collar

Next row (RS): K1, inc in next st, K to end.

Work 1 row.

Rep last 2 rows until there are 56 sts.

Cont straight until collar, unstretched, fits up left front slope to shoulder and across to centre back neck.

Cast off.

Slip st band and collar in place.

Mark positions for 5 buttons on this band – first to come level with buttonhole already worked in right front, last to come 1 cm below beg of front slope shaping, and rem 3 buttons evenly spaced between.

Buttonhole band and right collar

Slip 8 sts from right front holder onto 3¼mm (US 3) needles and rejoin yarn with WS facing.

Cont in g st until band, when slightly stretched, fits up right front opening edge to beg of front slope shaping, ending with RS facing for next row and with the addition of a further 4 buttonholes worked to correspond with positions marked for buttons as folls:

Next row (buttonhole row) (RS): K3, K2tog, yfwd (to make a buttonhole), K3.

Shape for collar

Next row (RS): K to last 2 sts, inc in next st, K1.

Complete to match button band and left collar, reversing shapings.

Slip st band and collar in place, joining ends of bands at centre back neck.

Collar edging

Using 3.50mm (US E4) crochet hook, make 2 ch.

Row 1 (RS): 1 dc into 2nd ch from hook, turn.

Row 2: 1 ch (does NOT count as st), 2 dc into first dc, turn. 2 sts.

Row 3: 15 ch, 3 tr into 4th ch from hook, 4 tr into each of next 11 ch, 2 dc into next dc, 1 dc into last dc, turn.

Row 4: 1 ch (does NOT count as st), 1 dc into each of first 2 dc, 2 dc into next dc, turn. 4 sts.

Cont in patt as folls:

Row 1 (RS): 1 ch (does NOT count as st), 1 dc into each of next 4 dc, turn.

Row 2: As row 1.

Row 3: 15 ch, 3 tr into 4th ch from hook, 4 tr into each of next 11 ch, 1 dc into each of next 4 dc, turn.

Row 4: As row 1.

These 4 rows form patt.

Starting and ending level with start of collar shaping, cont in patt until edging fits around outer edge of collar, ending after row 1 and with **WS** facing for next row.

Next row (WS): 1 ch (does NOT count as st), 1 dc into each of first 2 dc, dc2tog over last 2 dc, turn. 3 sts.

Next row: 15 ch, 3 tr into 4th ch from hook, 4 tr into each of next 11 ch, dc2tog over next 2 sts, 1 dc into last dc, turn.

Next row: 1 ch (does NOT count as st), dc2tog over first 2 sts.

Fasten off.

Sew straight edge of edging in place, starting and ending level with start of collar shaping and easing in slight fullness.

See information page for finishing instructions, setting in sleeves using the set-in method.

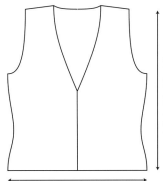

50 [51: 52: 53: 54] cm (19.5 [20: 20.5: 21: 21.5] in)

43 [46: 48.5: 51.5: 54] cm (17 [18: 19: 20.5: 21.5] in)

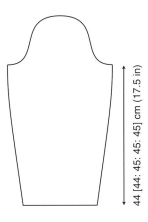

44 [44: 45: 45: 45] cm (17.5 in)

Tiffany

YARN

	XS	S	M	L	XL	
To fit bust	81	86	91	97	102	cm
	32	34	36	38	40	in

RYC Cashsoft DK

	10	11	11	12	12	x 50gm

(photographed in Mirage 503)

CROCHET HOOK

3.50mm (no 9) (US E4) crochet hook

TENSION

20 sts and 10 rows to 10 cm measured over treble pattern using 3.50mm (US E4) crochet hook.

CROCHET ABBREVIATIONS

ch = chain; **ss** = slip stitch; **dc** = double crochet; **htr** = half treble; **tr** = treble; **dtr** = double treble; **sp(s)** = space(s); **tr2tog** = (yoh and insert hook as indicated, yoh and draw loop through, yoh and draw through 2 loops) twice, yoh and draw through all 3 loops on hook; **tr3tog** = (yoh and insert hook as indicated, yoh and draw loop through, yoh and draw through 2 loops) 3 times, yoh and draw through all 4 loops on hook; **cluster** = (yoh and insert hook as indicated, yoh and draw loop through, yoh and draw through 2 loops) 5 times, yoh and draw through first 5 loops on hook, yoh and draw through rem 2 loops on hook; **yoh** = yarn over hook.

BACK

Using 3.50mm (US E4) hook, make 88 [92: 98: 102: 108] ch and fasten off.
Break yarn.
Miss first 30 ch, rejoin yarn to next ch and cont as folls:
Row 1 (RS): 1 ch (does NOT count as st), 1 dc into ch where yarn was rejoined, 1 dc into each of next 2 ch, 1 htr into each of next 3 ch, 1 tr into each of next 16 [20: 26: 30: 36] ch, 1 htr into each of next 3 ch, 1 dc into each of next 3 ch, 1 ss into each of next 6 ch, turn.
Row 2: 1 ch (does NOT count as st), 1 dc into each of first 3 ss, 1 htr into each of next 3 ss, 1 tr into each of next 28 [32: 38: 42: 48] sts, 1 htr into each of next 3 ch, 1 dc into each of next 3 ch, 1 ss into each of next 6 ch, turn.

Row 3: 1 ch (does NOT count as st), 1 dc into each of first 3 ss, 1 htr into each of next 3 ss, 1 tr into each of next 40 [44: 50: 54: 60] sts, 1 htr into each of next 3 ch, 1 dc into each of next 3 ch, 1 ss into each of next 6 ch, turn.
Row 4: 1 ch (does NOT count as st), 1 dc into each of first 3 ss, 1 htr into each of next 3 ss, 1 tr into each of next 52 [56: 62: 66: 72] sts, 1 htr into each of next 3 ch, 1 dc into each of next 3 ch, 1 ss into each of next 6 ch, turn.
Row 5: 1 ch (does NOT count as st), 1 dc into each of first 3 ss, 1 htr into each of next 3 ss, 1 tr into each of next 64 [68: 74: 78: 84] sts, 1 htr into each of next 3 ch, 1 dc into each of next 3 ch, 1 ss into each of next 6 ch, turn.
Row 6: 1 ch (does NOT count as st), 1 dc into each of first 3 ss, 1 htr into each of next 3 ss, 1 tr into each of next 76 [80: 86: 90: 96] sts, 1 htr into each of next 3 ch, 1 dc into each of last 3 ch, turn.
Row 7 (RS): 3 ch (counts as first tr), miss st at base of 3 ch, 1 tr into each st to end, turn. 88 [92: 98: 102: 108] sts.
Row 8: 3 ch (counts as first tr), miss st at base of 3 ch, 1 tr into each st to end, working last tr into top of 3 ch at beg of previous row, turn.
Row 8 forms tr patt.
Work in patt for 1 row.
Row 10: 3 ch (counts as first tr), miss tr at base of 3 ch, tr2tog over next 2 tr – one st decreased, 1 tr into each tr to last 3 sts, tr2tog over next 2 tr – one st decreased, 1 tr into top of 3 ch at beg of previous row, turn.
Dec 1 st at each end of 2nd and foll alt row.
82 [86: 92: 96: 102] sts.
Work in patt for 4 rows.
Row 19 (RS): 3 ch (counts as first tr), 1 tr into st at base of 3 ch – one st increased, 1 tr into each tr to last st, 2 tr into top of 3 ch at beg of previous row – one st increased, turn.
Inc 1 st at each end of 4th and foll 4th row.
88 [92: 98: 102: 108] sts.
Cont straight in patt until Back meas 33 cm **at centre**, ending with RS facing for next row.
Shape raglan armholes
Next row (RS): Ss across and into 4th st, 3 ch (counts as first tr), miss tr at base of 3 ch, 1 tr into each tr to last 3 sts and turn, leaving last 3 sts unworked. 82 [86: 92: 96: 102] sts.

Next row: 3 ch (counts as first tr), miss tr at base of 3 ch, tr3tog over next 3 sts - 2 sts decreased, 1 tr into each tr to last 4 sts, tr3tog over next 3 tr - 2 sts decreased, 1 tr into top of 3 ch at beg of previous row, turn.
Dec 2 sts at each end of next 2 [3: 5: 6: 8] rows.
70 [70: 68: 68: 66] sts.
Dec 1 st at each end of next 16 [15: 14: 13: 12] rows.
38 [40: 40: 42: 42] sts.
Fasten off.

FRONT

Work as given for Back to beg of raglan armhole shaping, ending with RS facing for next row.
Shape raglan armholes and divide for front opening
Next row (RS): Ss across and into 4th st, 3 ch (counts as first tr), miss tr at base of 3 ch, 1 tr into each of next 37 [39: 42: 44: 47] tr, turn, leaving rem sts unworked. 38 [40: 43: 45: 48] sts.
Dec 2 sts at raglan armhole edge of next 3 [4: 6: 7: 9] rows, then 1 st at raglan armhole edge of foll 9 [8: 7: 6: 5] rows **and at same time** dec 1 st at front opening edge on 2nd and every foll alt row.
17 [18: 18: 19: 18] sts.
Shape neck
XS, S and XL sizes
Next row (WS): Ss across and into 6th [7th: -: -: 7th] st, 3 ch (counts as first tr), miss tr at base of 3 ch, 1 tr into each tr to last 3 sts, tr2tog over next 2 sts, 1 tr into top of 3 ch at beg of previous row, turn. 11 sts.

M and L sizes
Next row (RS): 3 ch (counts as first tr), miss tr at base of 3 ch, tr2tog over next 2 sts, 1 tr into each of next 9 tr, turn. 11 sts.

All sizes
Dec 1 st at each end of next 3 rows, then dec 1 st at armhole edge **only** on foll 3 rows. 2 sts.
Fasten off.
With RS facing, return to last complete row worked, miss centre 6 sts, rejoin yarn to next st and cont as folls:
Next row (RS): 3 ch (counts as first tr), miss tr at base of 3 ch, 1 tr into each of next 37 [39: 42: 44: 47] tr, turn, leaving rem 3 sts unworked.
38 [40: 43: 45: 48] sts.
Complete to match first side, reversing shapings.

SLEEVES

Using 3.50mm (US E4) hook, make 54 [54: 58: 58: 62] ch.

Row 1 (RS): 1 tr into 4th ch from hook, 1 tr into each ch to end, turn. 52 [52: 56: 56: 60] sts.

Cont in tr patt as given for back, shaping sides by inc 1 st at each end of 4th and every foll 4th row until there are 64 [64: 68: 68: 72] sts.

Cont straight until sleeve meas 30 [30: 31: 31: 31] cm.

Shape raglan

Next row: Ss across and into 4th st, 3 ch (counts as first tr), miss tr at base of 3 ch, 1 tr into each tr to last 3 sts and turn, leaving last 3 sts unworked. 58 [58: 62: 62: 66] sts.

Dec 2 sts at each end of next 6 [6: 7: 7: 8] rows, then 1 st at each end of foll 13 rows. 8 sts.
Fasten off.

MAKING UP

Press as described on the information page.
Join raglan seams. Join side and sleeve seams.

Hem Border

With RS facing and 3.50mm (US E4) hook, rejoin yarn at base of one side seam, 1 ch (does NOT count as st), work 1 round of dc evenly around entire lower edge of Back and Front, working a multiple of 6 sts and ending with ss to first dc, turn.

Round 1 (WS): 1 ch (does NOT count as st), *1 dtr into next dc, 1 dc into next dc, rep from * to end, ss to top of first dtr, turn.

Round 2: 3 ch (does NOT count as st), *1 cluster into next dtr, 1 ch, miss 1 dc, rep from * to end, ss to top of first cluster, turn.

Round 3: 1 ch (does NOT count as st), *1 dc into next cluster, 1 dc into next ch sp, 1 dc into next cluster, 3 ch, ss to top of dc just worked, 1 dc into next ch sp, 1 dc into next cluster, 1 dc into next ch sp, 3 ch, ss to top of dc just worked, rep from * to end, ss to first dc.
Fasten off.

Cuff Borders

Work as for hem border, rejoining yarn at base of sleeve seam.

Neck Border

With RS facing and 3.50mm (US E4) hook, rejoin yarn at base of right front edge of front opening, 1 ch (does NOT count as st), work 1 row of dc evenly up right front opening edge, around neck edge and down left front opening edge to base of opening, working 5 dc into each front neck corner and ensuring there is a multiple of 6 sts plus 1, turn.

Row 1 (WS): 1 ch (does NOT count as st), *1 dtr into next dc, 1 dc into next dc, rep from * to last st, 1 dtr into last dc, turn.

Row 2: 3 ch (does NOT count as st), *1 cluster into next dtr, 1 ch, miss 1 dc, rep from * to last st, 1 cluster into last dtr, turn.

Row 3: 1 ch (does NOT count as st), *1 dc into next cluster, 1 dc into next ch sp, 3 ch, ss to top of dc just worked, 1 dc into next cluster, 1 dc into next ch sp, 1 dc into next cluster, 3 ch, ss to top of dc just worked, 1 dc into next ch sp, rep from * to last st, 1 dc into last cluster.
Fasten off.

Sew row-end edges of neck border to base of front opening.

See information page for finishing instructions.

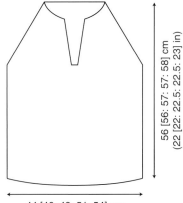

56 [56: 57: 57: 58] cm
(22 [22: 22.5: 22.5: 23] in)

44 [46: 49: 51: 54] cm
(17.5 [18: 19.5: 20: 21.5] in)

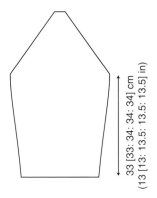

33 [33: 34: 34: 34] cm
(13 [13: 13.5: 13.5: 13.5] in)

YARN

	XS	S	M	L	XL	
To fit bust	81	86	91	97	102	cm
	32	34	36	38	40	in

RYC Cashsoft DK

	8	9	9	10	10	x 50gm

(photographed in Ballad Blue 508)

NEEDLES

1 pair 3¼mm (no 10) (US 3) needles
1 pair 4mm (no 8) (US 6) needles

BUTTONS – 10 x 75322

TENSION

22 sts and 30 rows to 10 cm measured over stocking stitch using 4mm (US 6) needles.

BACK

Using 3¼mm (US 3) needles cast on 81 [87: 93: 99: 105] sts.
Row 1 (RS): P1 [0: 1: 0: 1], *K1, P1, rep from * to last 0 [1: 0: 1: 0] st, K0 [1: 0: 1: 0].
Row 2: K1 [0: 1: 0: 1], *P1, K1, rep from * to last 0 [1: 0: 1: 0] st, P0 [1: 0: 1: 0].
These 2 rows form rib.
Cont in rib for a further 42 rows, ending with RS facing for next row.
Change to 4mm (US 6) needles.
Beg with a K row, cont in st st, shaping side seams by inc 1 st at each end of 5th and every foll 6th row until there are
95 [101: 107: 113: 119] sts.
Cont straight until back meas 30 cm, ending with RS facing for next row.
Shape raglan armholes
Cast off 2 sts at beg of next 2 rows.
91 [97: 103: 109: 115] sts.
XS size
Next row (RS): K1, sl 1, K1, psso, K to last 3 sts, K2tog, K1. 89 sts.
Next row: K1, P to last st, K1.
Next row: Knit.
Next row: K1, P to last st, K1.
M, L and XL sizes
Next row (RS): K1, sl 1, K2tog, psso, K to last 4 sts, K3tog, K1.
Next row: K1, P to last st, K1.

Rep last 2 rows – [-: 1: 2: 4] times more.
- [-: 95: 97: 95] sts.
All sizes
Next row (RS): K1, sl 1, K1, psso, K to last 3 sts, K2tog, K1.
Next row: K1, P to last st, K1.
Rep last 2 rows 30 [33: 32: 32: 31] times more, ending with RS facing for next row.
Cast off rem 27 [29: 29: 31: 31] sts.

POCKET LININGS (make 2)

Using 3¼mm (US 3) needles cast on 33 sts.
Row 1 (RS): K1, *P1, K1, rep from * to end.
Row 2: P1, *K1, P1, rep from * to end.
These 2 rows form rib.
Cont in rib for a further 42 rows, ending with RS facing for next row.
Break yarn and leave sts on a holder.

LEFT FRONT

Using 3¼mm (US 3) needles cast on 50 [53: 56: 59: 62] sts.
Row 1 (RS): P1 [0: 1: 0: 1], *K1, P1, rep from * to last st, K1.
Row 2: *P1, K1, rep from * to last 0 [1: 0: 1: 0] st, P0 [1: 0: 1: 0].
These 2 rows form rib.
Cont in rib for a further 41 rows, ending with **WS** facing for next row.
Place pocket
Row 44 (WS): Rib 9 and leave these sts onto a holder, rib 5 [5: 7: 7: 9], cast off next 33 sts in rib, rib to end.
Change to 4mm (US 6) needles.
Place pocket lining
Row 45 (RS): K3 [6: 7: 10: 11], K across 33 sts of first pocket lining, K to end.
41 [44: 47: 50: 53] sts.
Beg with a P row, cont in st st, shaping side seams by inc 1 st at beg of 4th and every foll 6th row until there are 48 [51: 54: 57: 60] sts.
Cont straight until left front matches back to beg of raglan armhole shaping, ending with RS facing for next row.
Shape raglan armhole
Cast off 2 sts at beg of next row.
46 [49: 52: 55: 58] sts.
Work 1 row.

XS size
Next row (RS): K1, sl 1, K1, psso, K to end.
45 sts.
Next row: P to last st, K1.
Next row: Knit.
Next row: P to last st, K1.
M, L and XL sizes
Next row (RS): K1, sl 1, K2tog, psso, K to end.
Next row: P to last st, K1.
Rep last 2 rows - [-: 1: 2: 4] times more.
- [-: 48: 49: 48] sts.
All sizes
Next row (RS): K1, sl 1, K1, psso, K to end.
Next row: P to last st, K1.
Rep last 2 rows until 22 [23: 23: 25: 25] sts rem, ending with **WS** facing for next row.
Shape neck
Cast off 4 [5: 5: 5: 5] sts at beg of next row.
18 [18: 18: 20: 20] sts.
Working all raglan armhole decreases as set, dec 1 st at each end of next and every foll alt row until 4 sts rem.
Work 1 row, ending with RS facing for next row.
Next row (RS): K1, sl 1, K2tog, psso.
Next row: P2.
Next row: K2tog and fasten off.

RIGHT FRONT

Using 3¼mm (US 3) needles cast on 50 [53: 56: 59: 62] sts.
Row 1 (RS): *K1, P1, rep from * to last 0 [1: 0: 1: 0] st, K0 [1: 0: 1: 0].
Row 2: K1 [0: 1: 0: 1], *P1, K1, rep from * to last st, P1.
These 2 rows form rib.
Cont in rib for a further 2 rows, ending with RS facing for next row.
Row 5 (RS): Rib 3, sl 1, K1, psso, yfwd (to make a buttonhole), rib to end.
Work 17 rows.
Row 23: As row 5.
Work 17 rows.
Row 41: As row 5.
Work 2 rows, ending with **WS** facing for next row.
Place pocket
Row 44 (WS): Rib 3 [6: 7: 10: 11], cast off next 33 sts in rib, rib 5 [5: 7: 7: 9] and turn, leaving rem 9 sts on a holder.
Change to 4mm (US 6) needles.

Place pocket lining

Row 45 (RS): K5 [5: 7: 7: 9], K across 33 sts of second pocket lining, K to end.
41 [44: 47: 50: 53] sts.
Beg with a P row, cont in st st, shaping side seams by inc 1 st at end of 4th and every foll 6th row until there are 48 [51: 54: 57: 60] sts.
Complete to match left front, reversing shapings, working an extra row before beg of raglan armhole and neck shaping.

SLEEVES

Using 3¼mm (US 3) needles cast on 51 [51: 53: 55: 55] sts.
Work in rib as given for pocket linings for 28 rows, ending with RS facing for next row.
Change to 4mm (US 6) needles.
Beg with a K row, cont in st st, shaping sides by inc 1 st at each end of 7th [7th: 7th: 7th: 5th] and every foll 8th [8th: 8th: 8th: 6th] row to 65 [75: 75: 77: 61] sts, then on every foll 10th [-: 10th: 10th: 8th] row until there are 73 [-: 77: 79: 81] sts.
Cont straight until sleeve meas 46 [46: 47: 47: 47] cm, ending with RS facing for next row.

Shape raglan

Cast off 2 sts at beg of next 2 rows.
69 [71: 73: 75: 77] sts.
Working all raglan decreases as set by back raglans, dec 1 st at each end of next and every foll alt row until 5 sts rem.
Work 1 row, ending with RS facing for next row.
Cast off rem 5 sts.

MAKING UP

Press as described on the information page.
Join raglan seams using back stitch, or mattress stitch if preferred.

Button Band

Slip 9 sts from left front holder onto 3¼mm (US 3) needles and rejoin yarn with RS facing.

Cont in rib as set until band, when slightly stretched, fits up left front opening edge to neck shaping, ending with RS facing for next row.
Break yarn and leave sts on a holder.
Slip st band in place.
Mark positions for 9 buttons on this band – first 3 buttons to come level with buttonholes already worked in right front, last will come just above neck shaping and rem 6 buttons evenly spaced between.

Buttonhole Band

Slip 9 sts from right front holder onto 3¼mm (US 3) needles and rejoin yarn with **WS** facing.
Cont in rib as set until band, when slightly stretched, fits up right front opening edge to neck shaping, with the addition of a further 6 buttonholes worked to correspond with positions marked for buttons as folls:
Buttonhole row (RS): Rib 3, sl 1, K1, psso, yfwd (to make a buttonhole), rib to end.
When band is complete, ending with RS facing for next row, do NOT break yarn.
Slip st band in place.

Neckband

With RS facing and using 3¼mm (US 3) needles, rib across 9 sts of buttonhole band, pick up and knit 19 [20: 20: 22: 22] sts up right side of neck, 5 sts from right sleeve, 27 [29: 29: 31: 31] sts from back, 5 sts from left sleeve, and 19 [20: 20: 22: 22] sts down left side of neck, then rib across 9 sts of button band.
93 [97: 97: 103: 103] sts.
Work in rib as set by bands for 3 rows, ending with RS facing for next row.
Next Row (buttonhole row) (RS): Rib 3, sl 1, K1, psso, yfwd (to make 10th buttonhole), rib to end.
Work a further 5 rows, ending with RS facing for next row.
Cast off in rib.
See information page for finishing instructions.

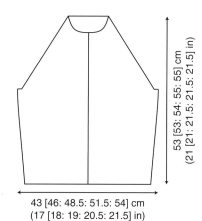

53 [53: 54: 55: 55] cm
(21 [21: 21.5: 21.5: 21.5] in)

43 [46: 48.5: 51.5: 54] cm
(17 [18: 19: 20.5: 21.5] in)

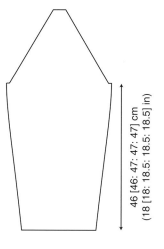

46 [46: 47: 47: 47] cm
(18 [18: 18.5: 18.5: 18.5] in)

Empire

YARN

	XS	S	M	L	XL	
To fit bust	81	86	91	97	102	cm
	32	34	36	38	40	in

RYC Cashsoft DK

	10	10	11	11	12	x 50gm

(photographed in Bella Donna 502)

NEEDLES

1 pair 3¼mm (no 10) (US 3) needles
1 pair 4mm (no 8) (US 6) needles
Cable needle

BEADS – approx 840 [850: 880: 890: 900] x
J3001008 beads

TENSION

22 sts and 30 rows to 10 cm measured over
stocking stitch using 4mm (US 6) needles.

SPECIAL ABBREVIATION

Bead 1 = place a bead by bringing yarn to RS of
work and slipping bead up next to st just worked,
slip next st purlwise from left needle to right
needle and take yarn to WS of work, leaving bead
sitting on RS of work in front of slipped st. Do not
place beads on edge stitches of work as this will
interfere with seaming
C2F = slip next st onto cable needle and leave at
front of work, K1, then K1 from cable needle
C2B = slip next st onto cable needle and leave at
back of work, K1, then K1 from cable needle
Cr2R = **on RS rows**: slip next st onto cable needle
and leave at back of work, K1 tbl, then P1 from
cable needle; **on WS rows**: slip next st onto cable
needle and leave at back of work, K1, then P1 tbl
from cable needle
Cr2L = **on RS rows**: slip next st onto cable needle
and leave at front of work, P1, then K1 tbl from
cable needle; **on WS rows**: slip next st onto cable
needle and leave at front of work, P1 tbl, then K1
from cable needle

Pattern note: Before starting to knit, thread
beads onto yarn. To do this, thread a fine sewing
needle (one that will easily pass through the
beads) with sewing thread. Knot ends of thread
and then pass end of yarn through this loop.

Thread a bead onto sewing thread and then
gently slide it along and onto knitting yarn.
Continue in this way until required number of
beads are on yarn.

BACK

Using 3¼mm (US 3) needles cast on 82 [88: 94:
100: 106] sts.
Row 1 (RS): K0 [1: 0: 0: 0], P0 [2: 2: 1: 0], *K2, P2,
rep from * to last 2 [1: 0: 3: 2] sts, K2 [1: 0: 2: 2],
P0 [0: 0: 1: 0].
Row 2: P0 [1: 0: 0: 0], K0 [2: 2: 1: 0], *P2, K2, rep
from * to last 2 [1: 0: 3: 2] sts, P2 [1: 0: 2: 2],
K0 [0: 0: 1: 0].
These 2 rows form rib.
Cont in rib for a further 31 rows, ending with **WS**
facing for next row.
Row 34 (WS): Rib 13 [16: 19: 22: 25], *M1, rib 1,
M1, rib 2, M1, rib 1, M1, rib 9, rep from * 4 times
more, rib to end. 102 [108: 114: 120: 126] sts.
Change to 4mm (US 6) needles.
Beg and ending rows as indicated and rep the
16 row patt rep throughout, cont in patt from chart
for back, shaping side seams by inc 1 st at each
end of 9th and every foll 8th row until there are
116 [122: 128: 134: 140] sts, taking inc sts into patt.
Cont straight until back meas 32 [33: 33: 34: 34] cm,
ending with RS facing for next row.
Shape armholes
Keeping patt correct, cast off 4 [5: 5: 6: 6] sts at
beg of next 2 rows. 108 [112: 118: 122: 128] sts.
Dec 1 st at each end of next 5 [5: 7: 7: 9] rows,
then on foll 1 [2: 2: 3: 3] alt rows, then on every
foll 4th row until 92 [94: 96: 98: 100] sts rem.
Cont straight until armhole meas 20 [20: 21:
21: 22] cm, ending with RS facing for next row.
Shape shoulders and back neck
Cast off 5 [5: 5: 5: 6] sts at beg of next 2 rows.
82 [84: 86: 88: 88] sts.
Next row (RS): Cast off 5 [5: 5: 5: 6] sts, patt until
there are 9 [9: 10: 10: 9] sts on right needle and
turn, leaving rem sts on a holder.
Work each side of neck separately.
Cast off 4 sts at beg of next row.
Cast off rem 5 [5: 6: 6: 5] sts.
With RS facing, rejoin yarn to rem sts, cast off centre
54 [56: 56: 58: 58] sts dec 12 sts evenly, patt to end.
Complete to match first side, reversing shapings.

FRONT

Work as given for back until 12 [12: 12: 14: 14]
rows less have been worked than on back to beg
of shoulder shaping, ending with RS facing for
next row.
Shape neck
Next row (RS): Patt 22 [22: 23: 24: 25] sts and
turn, leaving rem sts on a holder.
Work each side of neck separately.
Dec 1 st at neck edge on next 3 rows, then on foll
4 [4: 4: 5: 5] alt rows, ending with RS facing for
next row. 15 [15: 16: 16: 17] sts.
Shape shoulder
Cast off 5 [5: 5: 5: 6] sts at beg of next and foll alt
row.
Work 1 row.
Cast off rem 5 [5: 6: 6: 5] sts.
With RS facing, rejoin yarn to rem sts, cast off
centre 48 [50: 50: 50: 50] sts dec 6 sts evenly, patt to end.
Complete to match first side, reversing shapings,
working an extra row before beg of shoulder
shaping.

SLEEVES

Using 3¼mm (US 3) needles cast on 50 [50: 52:
54: 54] sts.
Row 1 (RS): P0 [0: 1: 2: 2], *K2, P2, rep from * to
last 2 [2: 3: 4: 4] sts, K2, P0 [0: 1: 2: 2].
Row 2: K0 [0: 1: 2: 2], *P2, K2, rep from * to last
2 [2: 3: 4: 4] sts, P2, K0 [0: 1: 2: 2].
These 2 rows form rib.
Cont in rib for a further 31 rows, ending with **WS**
facing for next row.
Row 34 (WS): Rib 10 [10: 11: 12: 12], *M1, rib 1,
M1, rib 2, M1, rib 1, M1, rib 9, rep from * twice
more, rib to end.
62 [62: 64: 66: 66] sts.
Change to 4mm (US 6) needles.
Beg and ending rows as indicated and rep the
16 row patt rep throughout, cont in patt from
chart for sleeves, shaping sides by inc 1 st at
each end of 7th [5th: 5th: 5th: 5th] and every foll
8th [6th: 6th: 6th: 6th] row until there are 82 [68:
68: 70: 78] sts, then on every foll 10th [8th: 8th:
8th: 8th] row until there are 84 [86: 88: 90: 92] sts,
taking inc sts into patt.
Cont straight until sleeve meas 46 [46: 47:
47: 47] cm, ending with RS facing for next row.

Back chart

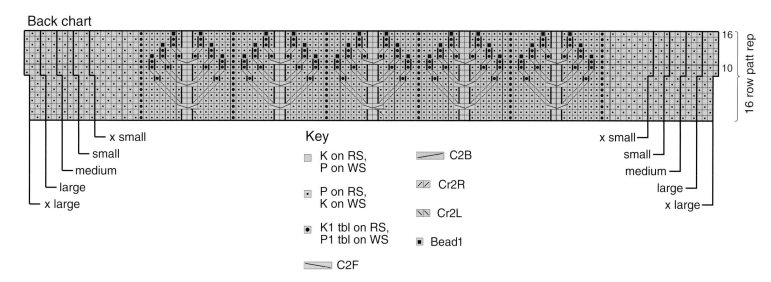

x small
small
medium
large
x large

x small
small
medium
large
x large

16
10

16 row patt rep

Key

▦	K on RS, P on WS	⬳	C2B
•	P on RS, K on WS	⧄	Cr2R
⊡	K1 tbl on RS, P1 tbl on WS	⧅	Cr2L
⬳	C2F	■	Bead1

Shape top

Keeping patt correct, cast off 4 [5: 5: 6: 6] sts at beg of next 2 rows. 76 [76: 78: 78: 80] sts.
Dec 1 st at each end of next 5 rows, then on foll 2 alt rows, then on every foll 4th row until 50 [50: 52: 52: 54] sts rem.
Work 1 row, ending with RS facing for next row.
Dec 1 st at each end of next and every foll alt row to 42 sts, then on foll row, ending with RS facing for next row. 40 sts.
Cast off 5 sts at beg of next 2 rows.
Cast off rem 30 sts, dec 10 sts evenly.

MAKING UP

Press as described on the information page.
Join right shoulder seam using back stitch, or mattress stitch if preferred.

Neckband

With RS facing and using 3¼mm (US 3) needles, pick up and knit 14 [14: 14: 15: 17] sts down left side of neck, 36 [38: 38: 38: 38] sts from front, 14 [14: 14: 15: 17] sts up right side of neck, then 50 [52: 52: 54: 54] sts from back.
114 [118: 118: 122: 126] sts.
Row 1 (WS): P2, *K2, P2, rep from * to end.
Row 2: K2, *P2, K2, rep from * to end.
Rep last 2 rows twice more, then row 1 again.
Cast off in rib.

See information page for finishing instructions, setting in sleeves using the set-in method.

Sleeve chart

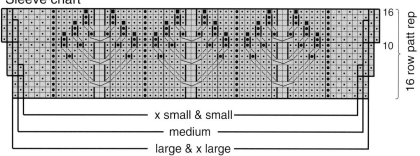

x small & small
medium
large & x large

16
10

16 row patt rep

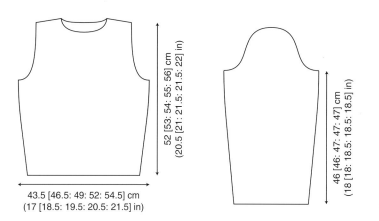

52 [53: 54: 55: 56] cm
(20.5 [21: 21.5: 21.5: 22] in)

43.5 [46.5: 49: 52: 54.5] cm
(17 [18.5: 19.5: 20.5: 21.5] in)

46 [46: 47: 47: 47] cm
(18 [18: 18.5: 18.5: 18.5] in)

Hamilton

YARN

		XS	S	M	L	XL	
To fit bust		81	86	91	97	102	cm
		32	34	36	38	40	in

RYC Cashsoft DK

A	Mist	505	4	4	4	5	5	x 50gm
B	Cream	500	3	3	3	3	3	x 50gm
C	Mirage	503	3	3	3	3	4	x 50gm

NEEDLES

1 pair 4mm (no 8) (US 6) needles (see pattern note below)
3.50mm (no 9) (US E4) crochet hook

TENSION

22 sts and 30 rows to 10 cm measured over stocking stitch using 4mm (US 6) needles.

CROCHET ABBREVIATIONS

ss = slip stitch; **dc** = double crochet; **ch** = chain; **sp** = space;

Pattern note: Striped st st patt is made up of blocks of yarn A and one row stripes of yarn B and C. To avoid repeatedly joining in and breaking off yarns, you may prefer to work on double-pointed or circular needles. Simply slide sts to end of needle where yarn needed next has been left and work row from that end, ensuring st st is kept correct. Take care when working shaping as it may NOT be worked at end of row specified in pattern, depending on point at which shaping falls within stripes.

BACK

Using 4mm (US 6) needles and yarn A cast on 95 [101: 107: 113: 119] sts.
Cont in striped st st patt (see pattern note) as folls:
Row 1 (RS): Using yarn A, knit.
Row 2: Using yarn A, purl.
Rows 3 to 6: As rows 1 and 2 twice.
Join in yarn B.
Row 7: Using yarn B, knit.
Join in yarn C.
Row 8: Using yarn C, purl.
Rows 9 to 16: As rows 7 and 8, 4 times.
These 16 rows form striped st st patt.
Keeping patt correct, dec 1 st at each end of 3rd and every foll 6th row to 87 [93: 99: 105: 111] sts,

then on every foll 4th row until 81 [87: 93: 99: 105] sts rem.
Work 9 rows, ending with RS facing for next row.
Inc 1 st at each end of next and every foll 6th row until there are 95 [101: 107: 113: 119] sts.
Cont straight until back meas 35 [36: 36: 37: 37] cm, ending with RS facing for next row.
Shape armholes
Keeping patt correct, cast off 4 [5: 5: 6: 6] sts at beg of next 2 rows. 87 [91: 97: 101: 107] sts.**
Dec 1 st at each end of next 3 [3: 5: 5: 7] rows, then on foll 2 [3: 3: 4: 4] alt rows, then on every foll 4th row until 73 [75: 77: 79: 81] sts rem.
Cont straight until armhole meas 20 [20: 21: 21: 22] cm, ending with RS facing for next row.
Shape shoulders and back neck
Cast off 7 [7: 7: 7: 8] sts at beg of next 2 rows. 59 [61: 63: 65: 65] sts.
Next row (RS): Cast off 7 [7: 7: 7: 8] sts, K until there are 11 [11: 12: 12: 11] sts on right needle and turn, leaving rem sts on a holder.
Work each side of neck separately.
Cast off 4 sts at beg of next row.
Cast off rem 7 [7: 8: 8: 7] sts.
With RS facing, rejoin yarns to rem sts, cast off centre 23 [25: 25: 27: 27] sts, K to end.
Complete to match first side, reversing shapings.

FRONT

Work as given for back to **.
Dec 1 st at each end of next 2 rows, ending with RS facing for next row.
83 [87: 93: 97: 103] sts.
Divide for neck
Next row (RS): K2tog, K39 [41: 44: 46: 49] and turn, leaving rem sts on a holder.
Work each side of neck separately.
Dec 0 [0: 1: 1: 1] st at armhole edge of next row. 40 [42: 44: 46: 49] sts.
Dec 1 st at armhole edge of next 1 [1: 1: 1: 3] rows, then on foll 1 [2: 3: 4: 4] alt rows, then on 2 foll 4th rows **and at same time** dec 1 st at neck edge of next and foll 5 [6: 6: 8: 7] alt rows, then on foll 0 [0: 0: 0: 4th] row.
30 [30: 31: 30: 31] sts.
Dec 1 st at neck edge **only** on 2nd [2nd: 2nd: 4th: 4th] and foll 0 [1: 0: 0: 0] alt rows, then on every foll 4th row until 21 [21: 22: 22: 23] sts rem.

Cont straight until front matches back to beg of shoulder shaping, ending with RS facing for next row.
Shape shoulder
Cast off 7 [7: 7: 7: 8] sts at beg of next and foll alt row.
Work 1 row.
Cast off rem 7 [7: 8: 8: 7] sts.
With RS facing, rejoin yarn to rem sts, K2tog, K to last 2 sts, K2tog.
Complete to match first side, reversing shapings, working an extra row before beg of shoulder shaping.

SLEEVES

Using 4mm (US 6) needles and yarn A cast on 51 [51: 53: 55: 55] sts.
Beg with patt row 5, cont in striped st st patt as given for back, shaping sides by inc 1 st at each end of 9th [9th: 9th: 9th: 7th] and every foll 10th [10th: 10th: 10th: 8th] row to 63 [71: 73: 73: 59] sts, then on every foll 12th [12th: 12th: 12th: 10th] row until there are 73 [75: 77: 79: 81] sts.
Cont straight until sleeve meas 45 [46: 46: 47: 47] cm, ending after same stripe row as on back to beg of armhole shaping and with RS facing for next row.
Shape top
Keeping stripes correct, cast off 4 [5: 5: 6: 6] sts at beg of next 2 rows. 65 [65: 67: 67: 69] sts.
Dec 1 st at each end of next 5 rows, then on every foll alt row to 21 sts, then on foll 3 rows, ending with RS facing for next row. 15 sts.
Cast off 3 sts at beg of next 2 rows.
Cast off rem 9 sts.

MAKING UP

Press as described on the information page.
Join both shoulder seams using back stitch, or mattress stitch if preferred.
Neck edging
With RS facing, using 3.50mm (US E4) crochet hook and yarn A, rejoin yarn at one shoulder seam, 1 ch (does NOT count as st), work 1 round of dc evenly around entire neck edge, working a multiple of 3 sts and ending with ss to first dc.
Next round (WS): *5 ch, miss 2 dc, 1 ss into next dc, rep from * to end.

Next round: *5 dc into ch sp, ss to next ss, rep from * to end.
Fasten off.
See information page for finishing instructions, setting in sleeves using the set-in method.
Work crochet edging around lower edge of sleeves and body in same way as for neck edging.

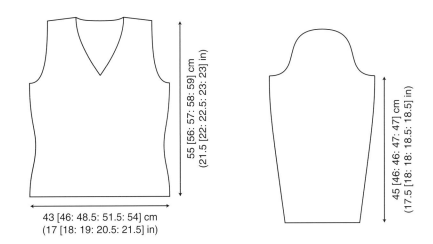

43 [46: 48.5: 51.5: 54] cm
(17 [18: 19: 20.5: 21.5] in)

55 [56: 57: 58: 59] cm
(21.5 [22: 22.5: 23: 23] in)

45 [46: 46: 47: 47] cm
(17.5 [18: 18: 18.5: 18.5] in)

 Broadway

YARN

	XS	S	M	L	XL	
To fit bust	81	86	91	97	102	cm
	32	34	36	38	40	in

RYC Cashsoft DK

	11	11	12	12	13	x 50gm

(photographed in Tape 515)

NEEDLES

1 pair 3¼mm (no 10) (US 3) needles
1 pair 4mm (no 8) (US 6) needles
Cable needle

BUTTONS – 6 x 75317

TENSION

22 sts and 30 rows to 10 cm measured over
stocking stitch using 4mm (US 6) needles.

SPECIAL ABBREVIATIONS

Tw3 = slip next 2 sts onto cable needle and leave
at front of work, K1 tbl, slip P st back onto left
needle and P this st, then K1 tbl from cable
needle

C6F = slip next 3 sts onto cable needle and leave
at front of work, K3, then K3 from cable needle
C6B = slip next 3 sts onto cable needle and leave
at back of work, K3, then K3 from cable needle
Cr8R = slip next 2 sts onto cable needle and
leave at back of work, K6, then P1, K1 tbl from
cable needle
Cr8L = slip next 6 sts onto cable needle and
leave at front of work, K1 tbl, P1, then K6 from
cable needle
Cr8RP = slip next 2 sts onto cable needle and
leave at back of work, K6, then P2 from cable
needle
Cr8LP = slip next 6 sts onto cable needle and
leave at front of work, P2, then K6 from cable
needle

BACK

Using 3¼mm (US 3) needles cast on 133 [139:
145: 151: 157] sts.
Row 1 (RS): K1 tbl, *P1, K1 tbl, rep from * to end.
Row 2: P1 tbl, *K1, P1 tbl, rep from * to end.
Rows 3 and 4: As rows 1 and 2.
Row 5: K1 tbl, *P1, Tw3, P1, K1 tbl, rep from * to end.

Row 6: As row 2.
These 6 rows form fancy rib.
Cont in fancy rib for a further 11 rows, ending with
WS facing for next row.
Row 18 (WS): Rib 7 [3: 6: 3: 6], work 2 tog, *rib 7
[8: 8: 9: 9], work 2 tog, rep from * to last 7 [4: 7:
3: 6] sts, rib to end. 119 [125: 131: 137: 143] sts.
Change to 4mm (US 6) needles.
Next row (RS): K5 [8: 11: 14: 17], P2, K6, P7, K6,
P1, K1 tbl, P1, K6, P7, K6, P2, K19, P2, K6, P7, K6,
P1, K1 tbl, P1, K6, P7, K6, P2, K5 [8: 11: 14: 17].
Next row: P5 [8: 11: 14: 17], K2, P6, K7, P6, K1,
P1 tbl, K1, P6, K7, P6, K2, P19, K2, P6, K7, P6, K1,
P1 tbl, K1, P6, K7, P6, K2, P5 [8: 11: 14: 17].
Place charts
Row 1 (RS): K5 [8: 11: 14: 17], work next 45 sts as
row 1 of chart, K19, work next 45 sts as row 1 of
chart, K5 [8: 11: 14: 17].
Row 2: P5 [8: 11: 14: 17], work next 45 sts as row
2 of chart, P19, work next 45 sts as row 2 of
chart, P5 [8: 11: 14: 17].
These 2 rows set the sts – 2 charts with st st
between and at sides.
Cont as set, repeating the 24 row chart patt rep
throughout, shaping side seams by inc 1 st at each
end of 7th and every foll 8th row until there are
129 [135: 141: 147: 153] sts, taking inc sts into st st.
Cont straight until back meas 24 [25: 25: 26: 26] cm,
ending with RS facing for next row.
Shape armholes
Keeping patt correct, cast off 4 [5: 5: 6: 6] sts at
beg of next 2 rows. 121 [125: 131: 135: 141] sts.
Dec 1 st at each end of next 3 [3: 5: 5: 7] rows,
then on foll 2 [3: 3: 4: 4] alt rows, then on every
foll 4th row until 107 [109: 111: 113: 115] sts rem.
Cont straight until armhole meas 20 [20: 21: 21:
22] cm, ending with RS facing for next row.
Shape shoulders and back neck
Cast off 12 [12: 12: 12: 13] sts at beg of next 2 rows.
83 [85: 87: 89: 89] sts.
Next row (RS): Cast off 12 [12: 12: 12: 13] sts,
patt until there are 16 [16: 17: 17: 16] sts on right
needle and turn, leaving rem sts on a holder.
Work each side of neck separately.
Cast off 4 sts at beg of next row.
Cast off rem 12 [12: 13: 13: 12] sts.
With RS facing, rejoin yarn to rem sts, cast off
centre 27 [29: 29: 31: 31] sts, patt to end.

Complete to match first side, reversing shapings.

LEFT FRONT

Using 3¼mm (US 3) needles cast on 67 [73: 73:
79: 79] sts.
Work in fancy rib as given for back for 17 rows,
ending with **WS** facing for next row.
Row 18 (WS): Rib 5 [4: 5: 2: 5], work 2 tog, *rib 7
[5: 8: 6: 9], work 2 tog, rep from * to last 6 [4: 6:
3: 6] sts, rib to end. 60 [63: 66: 69: 72] sts.
Change to 4mm (US 6) needles.**
Next row (RS): K5 [8: 11: 14: 17], P2, K6, P7, K6,
P1, K1 tbl, P1, K6, P7, K6, P2, K10.
Next row: P10, K2, P6, K7, P6, K1, P1 tbl, K1, P6,
K7, P6, K2, P5 [8: 11: 14: 17].
Place chart
Row 1 (RS): K5 [8: 11: 14: 17], work next 45 sts as
row 1 of chart, K10.
Row 2: P10, work next 45 sts as row 2 of chart,
P5 [8: 11: 14: 17].
These 2 rows set the sts – chart with st st at sides.
Cont as set, repeating the 24 row chart patt rep
throughout, shaping side seam by inc 1 st at beg
of 7th and every foll 8th row until there are
65 [68: 71: 74: 77] sts, taking inc sts into st st.
Cont straight until left front matches back to beg
of armhole shaping, ending with RS facing for
next row.
Shape armhole
Keeping patt correct, cast off 4 [5: 5: 6: 6] sts at
beg of next row. 61 [63: 66: 68: 71] sts.
Work 1 row.
Dec 1 st at armhole edge of next 3 [3: 5: 5: 7]
rows, then on foll 2 [3: 3: 4: 4] alt rows, then on
every foll 4th row until 54 [55: 56: 57: 58] sts rem.
Cont straight until 19 [19: 19: 21: 21] rows less have
been worked than on back to beg of shoulder
shaping, ending with **WS** facing for next row.
Shape neck
Keeping patt correct, cast off 8 [9: 9: 9: 9] sts at
beg of next row. 46 [46: 47: 48: 49] sts.
Dec 1 st at neck edge on next 6 rows, then on foll
2 [2: 2: 3: 3] alt rows, then on every foll 4th row
until 36 [36: 37: 37: 38] sts rem, ending with RS
facing for next row.
Shape shoulder
Cast off 12 [12: 12: 12: 13] sts at beg of next and
foll alt row.

Work 1 row.
Cast off rem 12 [12: 13: 13: 12] sts.

RIGHT FRONT
Work as given for left front to **.
Next row (RS): K10, P2, K6, P7, K6, P1, K1 tbl, P1, K6, P7, K6, P2, K5 [8: 11: 14: 17].
Next row: P5 [8: 11: 14: 17], K2, P6, K7, P6, K1, P1 tbl, K1, P6, K7, P6, K2, P10.
Place chart
Row 1 (RS): K10, work next 45 sts as row 1 of chart, K5 [8: 11: 14: 17].
Row 2: P5 [8: 11: 14: 17], work next 45 sts as row 2 of chart, P10.
These 2 rows set the sts – chart with st st at sides.
Cont as set, repeating the 24 row chart patt rep throughout, shaping side seam by inc 1 st at end of 7th and every foll 8th row until there are 65 [68: 71: 74: 77] sts, taking inc sts into st st.
Complete to match left front, reversing shapings, working an extra row before beg of armhole, neck and shoulder shaping.

SLEEVES
Using 3¼mm (US 3) needles cast on 79 [79: 79: 85: 85] sts.
Work in fancy rib as given for back for 17 rows, ending with **WS** facing for next row.
Row 18 (WS): Rib 3 [3: 6: 5: 5], work 2 tog, *rib 8 [8: 11: 6: 6], work 2 tog, rep from * to last 4 [4: 6: 6: 6] sts, rib to end. 71 [71: 73: 75: 75] sts.
Change to 4mm (US 6) needles.

Next row (RS): K13 [13: 14: 15: 15], P2, K6, P7, K6, P1, K1 tbl, P1, K6, P7, K6, P2, K13 [13: 14: 15: 15].
Next row: P13 [13: 14: 15: 15], K2, P6, K7, P6, K1, P1 tbl, K1, P6, K7, P6, K2, P13 [13: 14: 15: 15].
Place chart
Row 1 (RS): K13 [13: 14: 15: 15], work next 45 sts as row 1 of chart, K13 [13: 14: 15: 15].
Row 2: P13 [13: 14: 15: 15], work next 45 sts as row 2 of chart, P13 [13: 14: 15: 15].
These 2 rows set the sts – chart with st st at sides.
Cont as set, repeating the 24 row chart patt rep throughout, shaping sides by inc 1 st at each end of 5th [5th: 5th: 5th: 3rd] and every foll 12th [10th: 10th: 10th: 10th] row to 89 [85: 85: 87: 97] sts, then on every foll - [12th: 12th: 12th: -] row until there are - [91: 93: 95: -] sts, taking inc sts into st st.
Cont straight until sleeve meas 46 [46: 47: 47: 47] cm, ending with RS facing for next row.
Shape top
Keeping patt correct, cast off 4 [5: 5: 6: 6] sts at beg of next 2 rows.
81 [81: 83: 83: 85] sts.
Dec 1 st at each end of next 3 rows, then on foll 3 alt rows, then on every foll 4th row until 59 [59: 61: 61: 63] sts rem.
Work 1 row, ending with RS facing for next row.
Dec 1 st at each end of next and every foll alt row to 53 sts, then on foll 7 rows, ending with RS facing for next row.
39 sts.

Cast off 5 sts at beg of next 2 rows.
Cast off rem 29 sts, dec 6 sts evenly.

MAKING UP
Press as described on the information page.
Join both shoulder seams using back stitch, or mattress stitch if preferred.
Button Band
Using 3¼mm (US 3) needles cast on 10 sts.
Row 1 (RS): *K1 tbl, P1, rep from * to end.
Row 2: *K1, P1 tbl, rep from * to end.
Row 3: *P1, K1 tbl, rep from * to end.
Row 4: *P1 tbl, K1, rep from * to end.
These 4 rows form patt.
Cont in patt until band, when slightly stretched, fits up left front opening edge to neck shaping, ending with RS facing for next row.
Cast off in patt.
Slip st band in place.
Mark positions for 6 buttons on this band – first to come 1.5 cm up from cast-on edge, last to come just below neck shaping and rem 4 buttons evenly spaced between.
Buttonhole Band
Work to match button band, with the addition of 6 buttonholes worked to correspond with positions marked for buttons as folls:
Buttonhole row (RS): Patt 4 sts, work 2 tog, yrn, patt to end.
When band is complete, ending with RS facing for next row, cast off in patt.
Slip st band in place.

Key

☐ K on RS, P on WS	▨	Cr8R
▣ P on RS, K on WS	▨	Cr8L
▪ K1 tbl on RS, P1 tbl on WS	▨	Cr8RP
	▨	Cr8LP
▱ C6B		
▱ C6F		

Collar

With RS facing and using 3¼mm (US 3) needles, starting and ending halfway across top of bands, pick up and knit 32 [33: 33: 35: 35] sts up right side of neck, 30 [32: 32: 34: 34] sts from back, then 32 [33: 33: 35: 35] sts down left side of neck. 94 [98: 98: 104: 104] sts.

Beg with row 1, work in patt as given for button band until collar meas 12 cm from pick-up row. Cast off in patt.

See information page for finishing instructions, setting in sleeves using the set-in method.

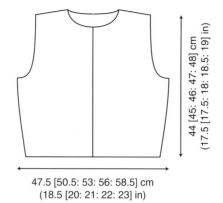

44 [45: 46: 47: 48] cm
(17.5 [17.5: 18: 18.5: 19] in)

47.5 [50.5: 53: 56: 58.5] cm
(18.5 [20: 21: 22: 23] in)

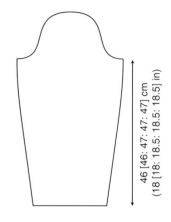

46 [46: 47: 47: 47] cm
(18 [18: 18.5: 18.5: 18.5] in)

Liberty

YARN

		XS	S	M	L	XL	
To fit bust		81	86	91	97	102	cm
		32	34	36	38	40	in

RYC Cashsoft DK and Cashcotton DK

			XS	S	M	L	XL	
A	Sft Mist	505	5	5	5	6	6	x 50gm
B	Sft Clementine	510	4	4	4	4	5	x 50gm
C	Cott Apple	603	2	3	3	3	3	x 50gm

NEEDLES

1 pair 3¼mm (no 10) (US 3) needles
1 pair 4mm (no 8) (US 6) needles
3¼mm (no 10) (US 3) circular needle

TENSION

22 sts and 32 rows to 10 cm measured over pattern using 4mm (US 6) needles.

SPECIAL ABBREVIATIONS

sL2P = slip next 2 sts purlwise one at a time
Cr3R = slip next 2 sts onto cable needle and leave at back of work, K1, then K2 from cable needle
Cr3L = slip next st onto cable needle and leave at front of work, K2, then K1 from cable needle
Cr4R = slip next 3 sts onto cable needle and leave at back of work, K1, then K3 from cable needle
Cr4L = slip next st onto cable needle and leave at front of work, K3, then K1 from cable needle

Pattern note: When working patt from chart, do NOT work slip sts on rows 13 and 14, 17 and 18, 25 and 26, and 29 and 30 if there will be insufficient sts to work crossed sts on rows 15, 19, 27 or 31. Instead, work these sts in st st.

BACK

Using 3¼mm (US 3) needles and yarn A cast on 93 [99: 105: 111: 117] sts.
Row 1 (RS): K1, *P1, K1, rep from * to end.
Row 2: P1, *K1, P1, rep from * to end.
These 2 rows form rib.
Cont in rib for a further 4 rows, inc 1 st at end of last row and ending with RS facing for next row. 94 [100: 106: 112: 118] sts.
Change to 4mm (US 6) needles.
Beg and ending rows as indicated and rep the

32 row patt rep throughout, cont in patt from chart, shaping side seams by dec 1 st at each end of 11th and every foll 8th row to 88 [94: 100: 106: 112] sts, then on every foll 6th row until 82 [88: 94: 100: 106] sts rem.
Cont straight until back meas 20 [21: 21: 22: 22] cm, ending with RS facing for next row.
Inc 1 st at each end of next and foll 8th row, then on every foll 10th row until there are 94 [100: 106: 112: 118] sts, taking inc sts into patt.
Work a further 9 rows, ending with RS facing for next row. (Back should meas 38 [39: 39: 40: 40] cm.)
Shape armholes
Keeping patt correct, cast off 4 [5: 5: 6: 6] sts at beg of next 2 rows. 86 [90: 96: 100: 106] sts.
Dec 1 st at each end of next 3 [3: 5: 5: 7] rows, then on foll 2 [3: 3: 4: 4] alt rows, then on every foll 4th row until 72 [74: 76: 78: 80] sts rem.
Cont straight until armhole meas 20 [20: 21: 21: 22] cm, ending with RS facing for next row.
Shape shoulders and back neck
Cast off 7 [7: 7: 7: 8] sts at beg of next 2 rows. 58 [60: 62: 64: 64] sts.
Next row (RS): Cast off 7 [7: 7: 7: 8] sts, patt until there are 11 [11: 12: 12: 11] sts on right needle and turn, leaving rem sts on a holder.
Work each side of neck separately.
Cast off 4 sts at beg of next row.
Cast off rem 7 [7: 8: 8: 7] sts.
With RS facing, rejoin yarns to rem sts, cast off centre 22 [24: 24: 26: 26] sts, patt to end.
Complete to match first side, reversing shapings.

LEFT FRONT

Using 3¼mm (US 3) needles and yarn A cast on 70 [74: 76: 80: 82] sts.
Row 1 (RS): *K1, P1, rep from * to end.
Row 2: As row 1.
These 2 rows form rib.
Cont in rib for a further 4 rows, inc 1 [0: 1: 0: 1] st at end of last row and ending with RS facing for next row. 71 [74: 77: 80: 83] sts.
Change to 4mm (US 6) needles.
Beg and ending rows as indicated, cont in patt from chart, shaping side seam by dec 1 st at beg of 11th and every foll 8th row to 68 [71: 74: 77: 80] sts, then on every foll 6th row until 65 [68: 71: 74: 77] sts rem.

Cont straight until 6 rows less have been worked than on back to first side seam inc, ending with RS facing for next row.
Shape front slope
Dec 1 st at end of next and foll 17 [19: 17: 19: 18] alt rows, then on 5 [4: 5: 4: 4] foll 4th rows **and at same time** inc 1 st at side seam edge on 7th and foll 8th row, then on every foll 10th row, taking inc sts into patt. 48 [50: 54: 56: 60] sts.
Dec 1 st at front slope edge **only** on 4th [4th: 4th: 4th: 2nd] and foll 4th row.
46 [48: 52: 54: 58] sts.
Work 1 [1: 1: 1: 3] rows, ending with RS facing for next row. (Left front should now match back to beg of armhole shaping.)
Shape armhole
Keeping patt correct, cast off 4 [5: 5: 6: 6] sts at beg and dec 0 [0: 0: 0: 1] st at end of next row.
42 [43: 47: 48: 51] sts.
Work 1 row.
Dec 1 st at armhole edge of next 3 [3: 5: 5: 7] rows, then on foll 2 [3: 3: 4: 4] alt rows, then on 2 foll 4th rows **and at same time** dec 1 st at front slope edge on next [next: next: next: 3rd] and every foll 4th row.
31 [30: 32: 31: 32] sts.
Dec 1 st at front slope edge **only** on 2nd [4th: 2nd: 4th: 4th] and every foll 4th row until 21 [21: 22: 22: 23] sts rem.
Cont straight until left front matches back to beg of shoulder shaping, ending with RS facing for next row.
Shape shoulder
Cast off 7 [7: 7: 7: 8] sts at beg of next and foll alt row.
Work 1 row.
Cast off rem 7 [7: 8: 8: 7] sts.
RIGHT FRONT
Using 3¼mm (US 3) needles and yarn A cast on 70 [74: 76: 80: 82] sts.
Row 1 (RS): *P1, K1, rep from * to end.
Row 2: As row 1.
These 2 rows form rib.
Cont in rib for a further 4 rows, inc 1 [0: 1: 0: 1] st at beg of last row and ending with RS facing for next row.
71 [74: 77: 80: 83] sts.
Change to 4mm (US 6) needles.

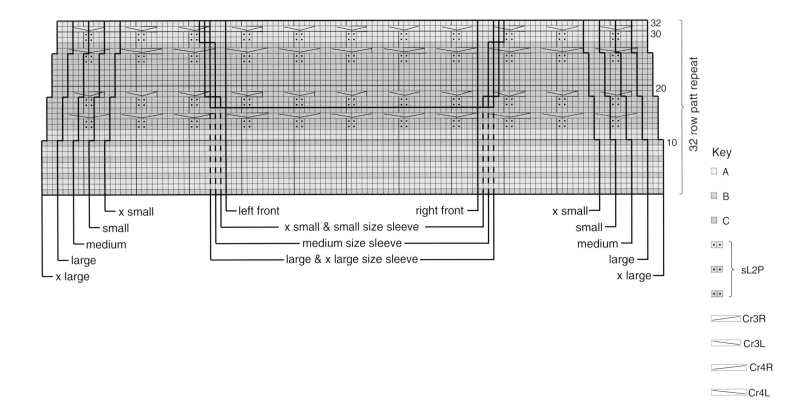

Key

☐ A
☐ B
☐ C

⊡ ⊡ ⊡ } sL2P

▱ Cr3R
▱ Cr3L
▱ Cr4R
▱ Cr4L

Beg and ending rows as indicated, cont in patt from chart, shaping side seam by dec 1 st at end of 17th and every foll 8th row to 68 [71: 74: 77: 80] sts, then on every foll 6th row until 65 [68: 71: 74: 77] sts rem.

Complete to match left front, reversing shapings, working an extra row before beg of armhole and shoulder shaping.

SLEEVES
Using 3¼mm (US 3) needles and yarn A cast on 49 [49: 51: 53: 53] sts.

Work in rib as given for back for 6 rows, inc 1 st at end of last row and ending with RS facing for next row.

50 [50: 52: 54: 54] sts.

Change to 4mm (US 6) needles.

Join in yarn C.

Using yarn C and beg with a K row, work in st st for 2 rows, ending with RS facing for next row.

Beg and ending rows as indicated and **beg with**

chart row 17, cont in patt from chart, shaping sides by inc 1 st at each end of 3rd and every foll 10th row to 54 [66: 64: 66: 78] sts, then on every foll 12th row until there are 72 [74: 76: 78: 80] sts, taking inc sts into patt.

Cont straight until sleeve meas approx 44 [45: 45: 46: 46] cm, ending after same patt row as on back to beg of armhole shaping and with RS facing for next row.

Shape top
Keeping patt correct, cast off 4 [5: 5: 6: 6] sts at beg of next 2 rows.

64 [64: 66: 66: 68] sts.

Dec 1 st at each end of next 3 rows, then on foll 3 alt rows, then on every foll 4th row until 40 [40: 42: 42: 44] sts rem.

Work 1 row, ending with RS facing for next row.

Dec 1 st at each end of next and every foll alt row to 34 sts, then on foll 7 rows, ending with RS facing for next row.

Cast off rem 20 sts.

MAKING UP
Press as described on the information page. Join both shoulder seams using back stitch, or mattress stitch if preferred.

Front band
With RS facing, using 3¼mm (US 3) circular needle and yarn A, starting at cast-on edge, pick up and knit 40 [42: 42: 44: 44] sts up right front opening edge to beg of front slope shaping, 95 [95: 97: 97: 99] sts up right front slope to shoulder, 30 [32: 32: 34: 34] sts from back, 95 [95: 97: 97: 99] sts down left front slope to beg of front slope shaping, then 40 [42: 42: 44: 44] sts down left front opening edge to cast-on edge.

300 [306: 310: 316: 320] sts.

Beg with a P row, work in st st for 3 rows, ending with RS facing for next row.

Row 4 (RS): Purl (to form fold line).

Beg with a P row, work in st st for 3 rows, ending with RS facing for next row.

Cast off.

Fold band in half to inside (along fold line row) and stitch in place.

See information page for finishing instructions, setting in sleeves using the set-in method and leaving a small opening in right side seam level with beg of front slope shaping.

Ties (make 2)

Using 3¼mm (US 3) needles and yarn A cast on 99 [110: 121: 132: 143] sts.

Beg with a P row, work in st st for 3 rows, ending with RS facing for next row.

Row 4 (RS): Purl (to form fold line).

Beg with a P row, work in st st for 3 rows, ending with RS facing for next row.

Cast off.

Fold Tie in half along fold line row and stitch along long edge and across one end. Attach open end to front opening edge, level with beg of front slope shaping.

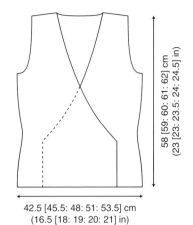

58 [59: 60: 61: 62] cm
(23 [23: 23.5: 24: 24.5] in)

42.5 [45.5: 48: 51: 53.5] cm
(16.5 [18: 19: 20: 21] in)

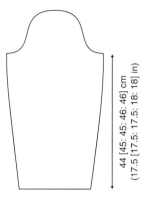

44 [45: 45: 46: 46] cm
(17.5 [17.5: 17.5: 18: 18] in)

AUSTRALIA
Australian Country Spinners,
314 Albert Street,
Brunswick,
Victoria 3056
Tel: (03) 9380 3888
Email: sales@auspinners.com.au

BELGIUM
Pavan, Meerlaanstraat 73,
B9860 Balegem (Oosterzele).
Tel: (32) 9 221 8594
Email: pavan@pandora.be

CANADA
Diamond Yarn,
9697 St Laurent,
Montreal,
Quebec, H3L 2N1.
Tel: (514) 388 6188

Diamond Yarn (Toronto),
155 Martin Ross,
Unit 3, Toronto,
Ontario,M3J 2L9.
Tel: (416) 736 6111
Email: diamond@diamondyarn.com
Web: www.diamondyarns.com

FINLAND
Oy Nordia Produkter Ab
Mikkolantie 1
00640 HELSINKI
Tel: (358) 9 777 4272
E-mail: info@nordiaprodukter.fi

FRANCE
Elle Tricot : 8 Rue du Coq,
67000 Strasbourg.
Tel: (33) 3 88 23 03 13.
Email: elletricot@agat.net.
Web: www.elletricote.com

GERMANY
Wolle & Design,
Wolfshovener Strasse 76,
52428 Julich-Stetternich.
Tel: (49) 2461 54735.
Email: Info@wolleunddesign.de.
Web: www.wolleunddesign.de

HOLLAND
de Afstap, Oude Leliestraat 12,
1015 AW Amsterdam.
Tel: (31) 20 6231445

HONG KONG
East Unity Co Ltd, Unit B2, 7/F Block B,
Kailey Industrial Centre,
12 Fung Yip Street, Chai Wan.
Tel: (852) 2869 7110
Fax: (852) 2537 6952
Email: eastuni@netvigator.com

ICELAND
Storkurinn, Laugavegi 59,
101 Reykjavik.
Tel: (354) 551 8258
Fax: (354) 562 8252
Email: malin@mmedia.is

ITALY
D.L. srl, Via Piave, 24 – 26,
20016 Pero, Milan.
Tel: (39) 02 339 10 180.

JAPAN
Puppy Co Ltd, T151-0051,
3-16-5 Sendagaya, Shibuyaku, Tokyo.
Tel: (81) 3 5412 7001
Email: info@rowan-jaeger.com

KOREA
De Win Co Ltd, Chongam Bldg,
101, 34-7 Samsung-dong, Seoul.
Tel: (82) 2 511 1087.
Email: knittking@yahoo.co.kr.
Web: www.dewin.co.kr

My Knit Studio, (3F) 121 Kwan Hoon Dong,
Chongro - ku, Seoul.
Tel: (82) 2 722 0006.
Email: myknit@myknit.com

NORWAY
Coats Norge A/S,
Postboks 63, 2801 Gjovik.
Tel: (47) 61 18 34 00
Fax: (47) 61 18 34 20

SINGAPORE
Golden Dragon,
315 Outram Road #06-03,
Tan Boon Liat Bldg, Singapore 169074.
Tel: (65) 6 220 3517.

SOUTH AFRICA
Arthur Bales PTY,
PO Box 44644, Linden 2104,
Tel: (27) 11 888 2401.

SPAIN
Oyambre, Pau Claris 145,
80009 Barcelona.
Tel: (34) 670 011957.
Email: comercial@oyambreonline.com

SWEDEN
Wincent, Norrtullsgatan 65,
113 45 Stockholm.
Tel: (46) 8 33 70 60
Fax: (46) 8 33 70 68
Email: wincent@chello.se
Web: www.wincentyarn.com

TAIWAN
Laiter Wool Knitting Co Ltd,
10-1 313 Lane,
Sec 3, Chung Ching North Road, Taipei,
Tel: (886) 2 2596 0269.

Long T eh Trading Co Ltd, 3F No. 19-2,
Kung Yuan Road, Taichung.
Tel: (886) 4 2225 6698.

Green Leave Thread Company, No 181,
Sec 4 Chung Ching North Road, Taipei,
Fax: (886) 2 8221 2919.

U.S.A.
Rowan USA, c/o Westminster
Fibers Inc, 4 Townsend West, Suite 8,
Nashua, New Hampshire 03063
Tel: (1 603) 886 5041 / 5043.
Email: rowan@westminsterfibers.com

U.K.
Rowan, Green Lane Mill, Holmfirth,
West Yorkshire, HD9 2DX.
Tel: 01484 681881.
Email: mail@knitrowan.com.
Web: www.knitrowan.com

For All Other Countries:
please contact Rowan for stockists details.